Julie Biuso's
never-ending
summer

For Remo, Luca and Ilaria,

not just for being great tasters, great supporters

and so much fun to be with,

but because you are all mine!

Julie Biuso's
never-ending
summer

Stunning barbecue dishes to tempt you all year round

Photography by Aaron McLean

NH
NEW
HOLLAND

6 introduction

8 setting up for the day
Sun's out! Hearty and wholesome or a tad indulgent, these are the sorts of things you might serve before midday, or thereabouts, eaten without rush or fuss.

24 something to start
Get the juices flowing! Small bites to quell your hunger before the main course; or choose several and make a meal of small plates of this and small tastes of that.

44 sandwiches, snacks and stacks
Well-made crusty bread – the smell makes you go weak at the knees – topped or stuffed with all manner of gorgeous titbits to eat as a snack or as a substantial meal.

66 things on sticks
Tasty morsels of food speared on bamboo sticks, rosemary stalks, lemon grass stems or lollipop sticks and cooked over the grill until sizzling, fragrant and utterly irresistible.

86 served in a bowl
Wok it, stir-fry it or stick it on the grill, add grains, pulses, salad or vegetables then serve in a bowl: fresh punchy flavours to arrest your palate.

106 food over flames
Seared, flamed or singed and cooked over a grill or on a griddle: scrumptiously good meat and fish dishes that will rock your taste buds.

contents

122 smart salads
The best barbecue deserves the best salad or side dish. In fact, some of these are so good, they may just steal the show.

136 sauces, salsas, dips and dunks
A spoonful here, a little drizzle there – these accompaniments add interest to all kinds of food as they unleash explosions of full-on flavour.

148 sweet endings
Too hard to resist! Fresh, fruity, smooth, chilling and thrilling, with the emphasis on fast: sweet mouthfuls to savour at the end of an outdoor feast.

160 know-how
160   barbecue tips
162   glossary and food tips

188 weights and measures

189 index

192 acknowledgements

introduction

Working on this book has made me feel good. It's a subject we all warmed to – and how could we not? Sea, sky and sand and all the gorgeousness that the outdoors offers, the smell of barbecued food wafting around inducing hunger, the chinking of glasses of cool rosé and sauvignon blanc . . . and they call this work!

This book started life as a companion to *Sizzle: Sensational barbecue food*, which had a successful run in the US, New Zealand, Australia, South Africa and England, and even got translated into French by Larousse! On its way it picked up a top international award from Gourmand for the Best Barbecue Book in the history of the awards. Writing a second similarly themed book seemed only fair to do it justice.

But as things went along *Never-ending Summer* metamorphosed into its own beast, as all good books do. I wanted to have the whole package – outdoor food, cooked on the grill, to be eaten morning, noon or night, food to take on a picnic to eat with your toes in the water, or to eat in your own back garden under a shady tree or in a sheltered spot as the sun sets. Food that will tempt, tease, surprise and please. Food with the *mmmmm* factor. And the back-up plan? That all the food could be cooked inside if the weather isn't behaving. I wanted side dishes and salads to round out the meal, stunning little numbers in their own right, and a choice of luscious or fuss-free desserts to finish it. I thought you might like to know approximately how long it takes to make and cook each dish. I wanted more than a collection of great, trusty recipes – I wanted to give the 'whys and hows', as many as would fit in the pages and more besides. The photography had to be real, lit with natural light, the food captured at its peak. I also thought a few video clips showing how to make star dishes would be a bonus (look for those recipes marked and go to www.juliebiuso.com for video clips as well as an extended glossary and more food tips).

So, this is it, still sizzling, still hot, food to be devoured enthusiastically in the great outdoors with family and friends, food to cook all year round, food to give pleasure, to stir the emotions. A collection of my favourite dishes all bursting with the yum-factor. Delicious dishes, dishes that are simply *just too good-looking to ignore!*

Julie Biuso

setting up for the day

Sun's out! Hearty and wholesome or a tad indulgent, these are the sorts

of things you might serve before midday, or thereabouts, eaten

without rush or fuss.

raisin bread with ricotta, honey and barbecued peaches

SERVES 6
TIME TO PREP 10 MINUTES
TIME TO COOK 5 MINUTES

THESE SWEET TOASTS CAN ALSO BE MADE WITH CROISSANTS OR SLICED BRIOCHE LOAF.

3 perfectly ripe free-stone peaches
70g thinly sliced prosciutto
1 small raisin or fruit loaf, sliced, or
**   sliced fruit bread**
100g ricotta
butter for hot plate
maple syrup or pouring honey
**   for serving**
fresh thyme sprigs for garnishing

1 Slice peaches into quarters, remove stones, and wrap each peach quarter in a little prosciutto.

2 Toast raisin loaf or fruit bread and arrange on individual plates. Top with spoonfuls of ricotta.

3 Cook peaches on a barbecue hot plate preheated to medium in a little sizzling butter until they take on some colour. Transfer peaches to a plate then put them on top of the ricotta. Drizzle everything with a little maple syrup or honey, and garnish with thyme. Serve immediately.

hash cakes

SERVES 4 AS A MAIN COURSE
TIME TO PREP 20 MINUTES
TIME TO COOK 25 MINUTES

I'VE USED SALAMI IN THESE HASH CAKES IN PLACE OF LEFTOVER
CORNED BEEF, AND THEY'RE ALL THE BETTER FOR IT.

1kg floury potatoes, such as agria
salt and freshly ground black pepper
1 bunch spring onions, trimmed and chopped
150g piece of salami, diced
1 tsp chopped thyme
1 small (size 5) free-range egg, lightly beaten
1 cup dried breadcrumbs (I use panko crumbs)
olive oil and butter for hot plate
butter
chutney for serving

1 Peel and cut potatoes into large chunks. Put potatoes in a saucepan, cover with cold water, salt lightly and bring to the boil. Lower the heat and cook gently for about 15 minutes, until tender when pierced with a skewer. Drain potatoes and return them to the wiped-out dry saucepan and set them back on the heat briefly to dry off clinging moisture. Mash potatoes by hand, adding half a teaspoon of salt. Set aside until cool.

2 Mix in spring onions, salami, thyme and plenty of freshly ground black pepper, then beat in the egg. Shape into small cakes then coat with breadcrumbs. Refrigerate until ready to cook.

3 Cook on a preheated oiled barbecue hot plate over medium–high heat. Fry until golden all over, dot the top of each cake with butter then turn them over with two spoons and cook the other side. Alternatively, cook them in a large frying pan in sizzling butter and oil. Serve hot with chutney.

banana hotcakes

SERVES 6 (MAKES 30)
TIME TO PREP 12 MINUTES
TIME TO COOK 7 MINUTES

MAKE THE HOTCAKES IN A SIZE TO SUIT – EITHER THREE SLICES OF
BATTER-COATED BANANA PER HOTCAKE, OR MAKE TINY HOTCAKES
WITH SINGLE SLICES OF BATTER-COATED BANANA. YUM!

1½ cups standard white flour
¼ tsp salt
1 tsp baking powder
1 tsp bicarbonate of soda
½ cup caster sugar
1 medium (size 6) free-range egg
1 cup milk
1 Tbsp melted butter, plus extra for hot plate
3 large bananas, peeled and sliced
icing sugar for serving
maple syrup for serving
grilled rashers of streaky bacon for serving

1 Sift flour, salt, baking powder and bicarbonate of soda into a bowl and make a well in the centre.

2 Put sugar, egg and milk in a jug and whisk together. Gradually pour into the dry ingredients, whisking as you go, to form a smooth batter. Add melted butter and sliced bananas and gently stir.

3 Cook in spoonfuls on a lightly buttered barbecue hot plate over medium heat. When bubbles form, flip hotcakes over and cook the other side. Keep warm on a plate covered with a thick tea towel while cooking the remainder. Alternatively, cook the hotcakes in a lightly greased frying pan over medium heat. Serve dusted with icing sugar with maple syrup and bacon on the side.

egg in the hole

SERVES 6
TIME TO PREP 5 MINUTES
TIME TO COOK 5 MINUTES

WHEN CRACKING THE EGGS, DISCARD ABOUT 50% OF THE EGG WHITE – A WHOLE EGG WILL BE TOO MUCH AND WILL OVERFLOW FROM THE HOLES. CO-ORDINATION IS EVERYTHING WITH THIS SIMPLE DISH. ENSURE ANY ACCOMPANIMENTS ARE COOKED AND READY TO SERVE BEFORE YOU BEGIN.

1 unsliced loaf grainy bread
butter, softened
6 small (size 5) free-range eggs
salt and freshly ground black pepper
rashers of grilled streaky bacon for serving, optional
small barbecued sausages for serving, optional
tomatoes, cooked on the barbecue hot plate or
    panfried, for serving, optional

1 Cut bread into 6 slices about 1.5cm thick. Butter bread on both sides, then use a small cutter to cut out circles from the centre of each slice.

2 Crack the eggs one by one into a small ramekin then transfer them carefully to a jug, taking care not to break the yolks. Put bread slices and small bread circles on the preheated barbecue hot plate and cook until golden. Flip bread slices over and carefully pour one egg into each cavity; use just enough egg white to fill the holes without overflowing them and discard the rest.

3 Cook eggs until done to your liking – it will take just a few minutes for set egg whites and runny yolks. Alternatively, heat a large non-stick frying pan over medium heat. Add as many slices of bread and bread circles as will fit in the pan and cook until golden. Flip them over and fill with egg as described. Season with salt and pepper and serve immediately with accompaniments of your choice.

fresh sausage rolls

SERVES 6
TIME TO PREP 10 MINUTES
TIME TO COOK 15 MINUTES

BOTH ROLLS AND SAUSAGES NEED TO BE SOFT FOR THIS COMBINATION TO WORK – CHEWY BREAD WILL BE DIFFICULT TO BITE THROUGH.

6 slim sausages
olive oil for hot plate
1 red pepper (capsicum)
1 medium-sized red onion, peeled and coarsely sliced
1½ Tbsp olive oil
salt and freshly ground black pepper
6 small round or oval bread rolls
butter, softened
creamy Dijonnaise mustard
chutney, optional
1 Tbsp chopped flat-leaf parsley for garnishing

1 Cook sausages on a preheated oiled barbecue hot plate over gentle heat until golden and cooked through. Alternatively, cook them in an oiled pan.

2 Halve pepper, remove core and seeds and slice finely. Heat oil in a saucepan over medium heat and add red onion and red pepper. Cook gently for about 10 minutes until nearly tender. Season to taste with a little salt and freshly ground black pepper.

3 Split the rolls lengthways through the top but not quite all the way through and spread with butter and mustard. Spoon a little red pepper and onion into each roll then slip in the sausages as soon as they are done. (The sausages can be sliced, if preferred.) Top each sausage with another spoonful of red pepper and onion and add a little chutney, if using. Season to taste with freshly ground black pepper, sprinkle with parsley and serve immediately.

apple buttermilk hotcakes

SERVES 5–6 (MAKES ABOUT 20)
TIME TO PREP 15 MINUTES
TIME TO COOK 15 MINUTES

THESE REALLY ARE THE BEST HOTCAKES: SERVED WITH SIZZLED APPLES, CRISPY BACON AND
MAPLE SYRUP, THEY'RE SIMPLY GORGEOUS.

2 cups standard white flour
pinch of salt
1½ tsp baking powder
**2 tsp caster sugar, plus extra for
  apples**
2 large (size 7) free-range eggs
500ml buttermilk
finely grated zest of 1 lemon
**2 Tbsp melted butter, plus extra
  for apples**
4 Granny Smith apples
**olive oil and butter for hot plate
  and frying**
**grilled rashers of streaky bacon
  for serving**
maple syrup for serving

1 Sift flour, salt and baking powder into a bowl and add the sugar. Separate eggs, putting egg whites in a clean grease-free bowl and the yolks in a jug. Add buttermilk and lemon zest to egg yolks and whisk together. Add melted butter.

2 Peel and grate two of the apples. Wrap in paper towels and squeeze to extract moisture. Add to buttermilk mixture.

3 Beat egg whites until stiff peaks form. Pour buttermilk mixture into dry ingredients and stir until just mixed. Fold in egg whites.

4 Cook hotcakes on a preheated oiled or buttered barbecue hot plate over gentle heat. Drop tablespoons of mixture onto hot plate and spread a little with a spoon to circles about 8 centimetres in diameter. Cook until golden brown underneath. Flip and cook the other side until golden. Transfer to a cake rack and keep warm covered with a clean tea towel while cooking remaining hotcakes. Alternatively, cook hotcakes in a large non-stick frying pan over medium heat.

5 Meanwhile, slice remaining apples thickly and dredge with caster sugar. Cook in a small non-stick pan in sizzling butter until golden. Serve hotcakes with bacon, apples and maple syrup.

quesadillas

SERVES 4–6
TIME TO PREP 15 MINUTES
TIME TO COOK 20 MINUTES

THIS IS KID'S STUFF WHICH THEY SHOULD BE ABLE TO COOK, TOO. I'D WRAP AN APRON
AROUND THEM ANY TIME FROM THE AGE OF FIVE ONWARDS AND GET THEM PEELING AND
CHOPPING, SIZZLING AND LAYERING. THEY'LL LOVE IT!

500g free-range pork sausages
   or leftover roasted free-range
   chicken
olive oil for hot plate
4–6 soft wheat flour or corn
   tortillas
1½ cups pre-grated mozzarella
   cheese
½ cup roughly chopped coriander
   leaves, plus extra for garnishing
½ cup canned sweet corn kernels,
   drained and squeezed dry in
   paper towels
¼ cup mild taco sauce
sour cream for serving
sliced fresh red chilli for serving

1 Split the sausages with a small sharp knife and remove and discard casings. Roughly chop sausage meat. Cook quickly on a preheated oiled barbecue hot plate over medium–high heat until browned on one side, breaking up sausage meat with a large fork. Turn sausage meat over and continue cooking until well browned and cooked through. Alternatively, cook in a medium-sized frying pan over medium heat. Drain off any fat. If using leftover roasted chicken, remove it from the bone, discard skin and fat, and chop coarsely.

2 Lay tortillas on a clean bench and put filling ingredients on one half of each: put cheese on first, then sausage meat (or chicken), coriander, sweet corn and a few dollops of taco sauce. Fold over to enclose the filling.

3 Cook tortillas on an oiled preheated barbecue hot plate over medium heat until golden. Turn and cook the other side until golden and the cheese has melted. Alternatively, cook in a hot sandwich press for several minutes. Cut into triangles and top with a dollop of sour cream and sliced chilli. Garnish with chopped coriander.

tomatoes with lemon zest

SERVES 3–4
TIME TO PREP 5 MINUTES
TIME TO COOK 5 MINUTES

THIS IS SUCH AN EASY TREATMENT FOR TOMATOES, BUT MAKE
SURE YOU CHOOSE FAIRLY FIRM TOMATOES SO THEY HOLD
TOGETHER. IF THEY LOOK LIKE THEY'RE COLLAPSING, JUST COOK
THEM ON ONE SIDE.

4 medium-sized vine tomatoes
finely grated zest of 1 lemon
1 tsp caster sugar
1 tsp sea salt
1 tsp freshly ground black pepper
olive oil for hot plate
basil leaves for garnishing

1 Slice tomatoes thickly and pat dry with paper towels.

2 Mix lemon zest and sugar together on a large dinner plate and add sea salt and freshly ground black pepper.

3 Dunk tomato slices in the lemony seasoning and cook them quickly on a preheated lightly oiled barbecue hot plate over medium heat until browned and fragrant. Alternatively, cook them in a non-stick frying pan over high heat. Garnish with fresh basil and serve immediately.

huevos con patatas

SERVES 4
TIME TO PREP 15 MINUTES
TIME TO COOK 40 MINUTES

THIS IS THE BEST HANGOVER CURE EVER – THAT MOREISH
COMBINATION OF FAT, CARBS AND SPICE WORKS EVERY TIME!

800g all-purpose potatoes, such as desiree, or agria or rua, peeled and finely diced
salt
3 Tbsp butter
1 x 410g can sweet corn kernels, drained
2 Tbsp chopped coriander leaves, plus extra for garnishing
1 small red onion, peeled and finely chopped
1 medium-sized tomato, diced
1 Tbsp lime juice
2–3 Tbsp hot Mexican chilli salsa, or to taste, plus extra for serving
1 fresh hot red chilli, finely chopped, optional
4 medium (size 6) free-range eggs
4 soft flour tortillas

1 Cook potatoes in gently boiling salted water. Lower the heat and cook until nearly tender. Drain, then tip onto a double thickness of paper towels to dry.

2 Put 2 tablespoons of butter in a heavy-based or non-stick frying pan and set it over medium heat. Add potatoes and cook for about 15 minutes, turning often, until golden. Alternatively, cook potatoes on an oiled and buttered barbecue hot plate.

3 Mix sweet corn, coriander, red onion, tomato, lime juice, salsa, a few pinches of salt and fresh chilli, if using, in a bowl. Break eggs into another bowl, keeping the yolks whole, and season with a little salt. Transfer potatoes to a plate. Wipe out pan, add 1 tablespoon butter and heat until sizzling. Pour in the eggs and fry until done to your liking.

4 Heat tortillas one at a time in a dry non-stick frying pan over medium heat until heated through. Put them on plates and distribute the potatoes and sweet corn salsa amongst them and top with the eggs. Serve more salsa on the side. Garnish with coriander.

crunchy potato cakes with avocado salsa

SERVES 6 OR MORE (MAKES 30 CAKES)
TIME TO PREP 30 MINUTES, PLUS 2 HOURS DRYING
TIME TO COOK 30 MINUTES

THESE ARE GREAT FOR BRUNCH OR AS AN ACCOMPANIMENT TO FISH OR BACON.

1 Peel and cut potatoes into large chunks. Put potatoes in a saucepan, cover with cold water, salt lightly and bring to the boil. Lower the heat and cook gently for about 15 minutes, until tender when pierced with a skewer. Drain potatoes and return them to the wiped-out dry pan and set the pan back on the heat briefly to dry off clinging moisture. Mash potatoes by hand. Beat in 1 egg and 1 teaspoon of salt, coriander, chilli and spring onions. Cover with a damp paper towel and leave at room temperature until cool.

2 Form mixture into small balls, then flatten slightly into small cakes.

3 Break two eggs into a bowl, add a few pinches of salt and beat with a fork. Pass potato cakes through beaten egg one at a time by resting them on a slotted spatula and spooning the egg over them. Let excess egg drip off, then coat them with crumbs, patting them on carefully. Let cakes dry for 2 hours before frying.

4 Make the salsa just before cooking the potato cakes. Halve and peel the avocados and remove the stones. Cut flesh into small pieces, transfer to a large bowl with the other ingredients and toss very gently.

5 Cook potato cakes on a preheated well oiled barbecue hot plate over medium heat until golden brown. Keep them sizzling by spraying with a little olive oil, or adding a little butter. Alternatively, cook potato cakes in a large frying pan in hot oil over medium heat. Drop in several potato cakes and cook until golden brown. Turn carefully and cook second side until golden. Lift out with a slotted spatula and drain briefly on crumpled paper towels. Repeat with remaining potato cake mixture.

6 Serve potato cakes with avocado salsa on the side.

1kg floury potatoes, such as agria
salt
3 medium (size 6) free-range eggs
2 Tbsp finely chopped coriander leaves
1 fresh hot red chilli, halved, deseeded and finely chopped
2 spring onions, trimmed and very finely chopped
1½ cups fine dry breadcrumbs or panko crumbs
olive oil and butter for hot plate

AVOCADO SALSA
2 perfectly ripe but firm avocados
6 small vine tomatoes, chopped then drained for 10 minutes in a sieve
2 Tbsp chopped shallots
2 Tbsp lime juice
¼ tsp salt
1 Tbsp chopped coriander leaves

Go to www.juliebiuso.com
for a video clip of Julie
demonstrating this recipe.

something to start

Get the juices flowing! Small bites to quell your hunger before the

main course; or choose several and make a meal of small plates

of this and small tastes of that.

spicy prawns in green coats

SERVES 6
TIME TO PREP 30 MINUTES, PLUS 30 MINUTES MARINATING
TIME TO COOK 7–10 MINUTES

SEXY IS THE ONLY WAY TO DESCRIBE THESE SPICY, SUCCULENT, FINGER-LICKING AND
TOTALLY ADDICTIVE PRAWNS.

500g large green (raw) prawns
1 Tbsp lime juice
salt and freshly ground black
   pepper
fresh lemon grass leaves or 1 small
   banana leaf, cut into strips
toothpicks
olive oil for hot plate

SPICE PASTE
100g shallots, peeled and roughly
   chopped
5 cloves garlic, peeled and roughly
   chopped
6 raw or lightly toasted macadamia
   nuts
2 Tbsp coarsely grated ginger
3 fresh medium–hot long red
   chillies, halved, deseeded and
   roughly chopped
½ tsp ground turmeric
½ cup thick canned coconut cream
1 Tbsp grated palm sugar

1 If prawns are frozen, thaw them quickly in a sealed plastic bag immersed in
a sink of warm water. Remove the centre part of the shell from each prawn,
leaving the heads and tails intact. Using a small sharp knife, slice down the back of
each prawn and gently extract the red or black vein. Rinse prawns and pat dry with
paper towels. Put prawns in a bowl and massage with the lime juice and a little salt
and pepper. Wrap a lemon grass leaf or a strip of banana leaf around the middle of
each prawn. Secure with toothpicks.

2 Put spice paste ingredients in a blender (liquidiser) and blend to a fine purée.
Pour over prawns. Cover and marinate for 30 minutes at room temperature.

3 Cook prawns on a preheated lightly oiled barbecue hot plate over medium–
high heat, brushing or spraying with a little oil from time to time and scraping
down the hot plate, if necessary, to keep the marinade from catching. The prawns
can also be cooked in batches in an oiled frying pan over medium–high heat. Serve
prawns hot with fingerbowls and serviettes.

toasted asparagus rolls

SERVES 4 (MAKES 12)
TIME TO PREP 12 MINUTES
TIME TO COOK 12 MINUTES

ONCE YOU'VE TASTED THESE ASPARAGUS ROLLS YOU'LL GIVE THOSE SOGGY LITTLE WHITE
BREAD AND CANNED ASPARAGUS ROLLS A WIDE BERTH. THESE ARE SIMPLY GORGEOUS!
AND ANOTHER PLUS – THEY CAN BE PREPARED A FEW HOURS AHEAD PROVIDING THE
ASPARAGUS SPEARS ARE NICE AND DRY BEFORE YOU ROLL THEM UP.

1 Wash asparagus spears and plunge them into a saucepan of boiling well-salted water. Cook uncovered for 2 minutes, then drain and refresh with plenty of cold water, until they stop steaming. Gently shake off clinging water. Lay asparagus spears on two sheets of paper towels to drain.

2 Put 2 tablespoons of butter on a large plate and melt in a microwave, or put butter in a ramekin placed in a sink of hot water, stir in garlic, then tip it onto a plate. Coat asparagus spears with garlic butter and season with salt and pepper.

3 Mix the rest of the butter with the mustard, chives, a pinch of salt and a little black pepper. Remove crusts from bread and sprinkle bread slices with parmesan cheese. Lay asparagus on top and roll up, pressing to seal. Smear outside of asparagus rolls with seasoned butter.

4 Cook asparagus rolls on a preheated barbecue hot plate over gentle heat, turning often, until golden and crusty. Alternatively, cook in a non-stick frying pan over gentle heat, or in a toasted sandwich maker, until golden. Sprinkle with parmesan cheese and serve hot.

12 fat asparagus spears, bases trimmed
salt and freshly ground black pepper
90g unsalted butter, softened
1 small clove garlic, peeled and crushed
1 Tbsp Dijon mustard
1 Tbsp snipped chives
12 slices grainy bread
½ cup freshly grated parmesan cheese, plus extra to garnish

smoky aubergine purée

SERVES 4–6
TIME TO PREP 20 MINUTES
TIME TO COOK 30 MINUTES

SINGEING AUBERGINES RESULTS IN A NUTTY, SMOKY FLAVOUR.
DON'T WORRY ABOUT THE BLACKENED SKIN – IT'S EASILY PICKED
OFF. SERVE THIS AS A DIP WITH BREADS OR FLATBREADS.

1 large aubergine (eggplant)
2 Tbsp vegetable oil
½ tsp cumin seeds
small knob of fresh ginger, peeled
   and chopped
1 fresh green chilli, halved, deseeded and chopped
1 large onion, peeled and chopped
2 cloves garlic, peeled and crushed
½ tsp ground turmeric
½ tsp chilli powder
1 tsp ground coriander
200g vine tomatoes, roughly chopped and
   cores discarded
¼ tsp salt
2 Tbsp chopped coriander leaves

1 Rub whole aubergine with 1 tablespoon oil and cook on a preheated barbecue grill rack over high heat, turning often with tongs, until charred. Alternatively, char aubergine over a gas flame and turn with tongs as it blackens. Transfer aubergine to a shallow ovenproof dish and cook in an oven preheated to 250°C for 15 minutes, or until tender. Set aside until cool, then peel off blackened skin from one side of aubergine and scoop out the flesh; discard the skin. Chop flesh coarsely and leave to drain in a sieve for 10 minutes.

2 Heat the rest of the oil in a frying pan over medium heat and add the cumin seeds. When the seeds begin to smell fragrant and darken in colour, add ginger and green chilli. Fry for 1 minute, stirring, then add onion and fry for about 7 minutes until softened, stirring often. Add garlic and let it cook through for 1 minute, then add turmeric, chilli powder and ground coriander.

3 Turn off the heat and add the aubergine and stir through, then stir in the tomatoes. Season with salt, stir the coriander through and serve warm.

pesto dip with roasted red pepper and olives

SERVES 6
TIME TO PREP 20 MINUTES
TIME TO COOK 7 MINUTES

THIS IS A QUICK AND VERY TASTY DIP TO PREPARE. JUST THE THING
FOR LATE SUMMER WHEN BASIL IS IN ABUNDANCE.

¼ cup pine nuts
2 cups lightly packed fresh basil leaves
2 cloves garlic, peeled and crushed
50ml extra virgin olive oil
175g creamy feta, drained and crumbled
¼ cup freshly grated parmesan cheese
salt and freshly ground black pepper
1 red pepper (capsicum) for garnishing
12 kalamata olives, pitted and chopped,
   for serving
crusty bread, for serving

1 Put the pine nuts in a small dry frying pan and set pan over medium heat. Shake the pan occasionally and cook until lightly golden.

2 Put basil leaves, garlic and oil in the bowl of a food processor or blender (liquidiser) and blend until smooth. Add the feta and blend again until smooth, then add the pine nuts and process briefly until the nuts are roughly chopped; you don't want it turned into a paste so leave them a little bit chunky. Transfer the dip to a bowl and stir in parmesan, a pinch of salt and a little black pepper. Thin with a little warm water, if necessary.

3 Cook the pepper on a barbecue grill rack over high heat, turning often until charred. Alternatively, cook it over a gas flame. Transfer pepper to a plate, drape it with a paper towel and leave to cool. Remove blackened skin, core, seeds and membranes and discard. Don't wash the pepper or you will lose valuable flavour; simply rinse your fingers from time to time when they get sticky. Cut flesh into strips.

4 Serve the dip in a bowl garnished with red pepper and with olives alongside, accompanied by crusty bread.

gazpacho with avocado and prawns

SERVES 6
TIME TO PREP 50 MINUTES, PLUS SEVERAL HOURS CHILLING
TIME TO COOK 7 MINUTES

THE DEAL WITH CHILLED SOUPS IS THAT THEY MUST BE SERVED ICY COLD – THEN THEY'RE THRILLING, REVIVING AND, AFTER THE CHILL SUBSIDES, STRANGELY CALMING. SERVED AT ANY OTHER TEMPERATURE, AND THAT INCLUDES JUST COLD, THEY'RE ABOUT AS EXCITING AS SUCKING ON A DAMP DISH CLOTH.

1 small red onion, peeled
½ telegraph cucumber
1 x 400g can Spanish or Italian chopped tomatoes
1 slice stale sourdough bread, without too much crust
2½ Tbsp extra virgin olive oil
2 large cloves garlic, peeled and chopped
1 tsp smoked Spanish paprika (sweet)
1¼ tsp salt
1 medium-sized red pepper (capsicum), halved, deseeded, cored and finely chopped
2 Tbsp Spanish sherry or red wine vinegar
1 cup tomato juice, chilled

TOPPING
1 ripe but firm avocado
1 Tbsp lime juice
extra virgin olive or avocado oil
1 fresh hot red chilli, halved, deseeded and finely chopped
2 Tbsp chopped coriander leaves
6 large green (raw) prawns, thawed if frozen
olive oil for hot plate

1 Finely slice onion and soak in icy cold water for 15 minutes. Peel cucumber, cut flesh lengthways and scoop out the seeds with a pointy teaspoon. Chop flesh coarsely. Put tomatoes in a bowl and, using a teaspoon, scoop out as many seeds as possible and discard.

2 Fry the slice of bread in 1 tablespoon hot oil until crisp. Chop bread roughly and put it in a food processor with the garlic and the rest of the oil. Process to a paste.

3 Drain onion and add it to processor bowl along with the smoked paprika and salt. Blend until smooth. Add red pepper and blend again until smooth. Add cucumber and tomatoes and process until very smooth. Pass through a coarse sieve set over a bowl. Stir in sherry or vinegar and tomato juice, adding a little chilled water if necessary to thin the soup.

4 Cover and refrigerate gazpacho for several hours, then check the seasoning; it may need more salt.

5 Transfer gazpacho to the freezer at least 45 minutes before serving so that icy shards start forming around the sides of the bowl.

6 Meanwhile, make the topping. Halve avocado, remove stone and peel. Dice flesh finely, transfer to a shallow bowl, then sprinkle with lime juice and a splash of extra virgin olive or avocado oil. Sprinkle over chopped chilli and coriander. Cook prawns on a preheated oiled barbecue hot plate over high heat for 2–3 minutes each side. Alternatively, heat 1 tablespoon olive oil in a small pan over medium heat and when hot, drop in prawns. Cook quickly on both sides, just until the prawns change colour.

7 Ladle soup into bowls and put a spoonful of seasoned avocado and a prawn on top. Serve immediately.

pan-fried calamari with lemon pepper mayonnaise

SERVES 4
TIME TO PREP 25 MINUTES
TIME TO COOK 5 MINUTES

I'M NOT USUALLY ONE TO USE FROZEN SEAFOOD, BUT I HAVE MADE THESE SUCCESSFULLY WITH FROZEN CALAMARI RINGS.

MAYONNAISE

3 medium (size 6) free-range egg yolks, at room temperature
about ¼ tsp salt
¼ tsp Dijon mustard
300ml olive oil
1–2 Tbsp lemon juice
1 tsp freshly ground lemon pepper, or to taste

CALAMARI

350g small prepared calamari rings, fresh or frozen
olive oil for hot plate
2 cloves garlic, peeled and very finely chopped
1 Tbsp finely chopped flat-leaf parsley
1 Tbsp finely chopped rosemary
sea salt

1 To make the mayonnaise, whisk egg yolks, salt and mustard in a small bowl with a whisk until egg yolks darken and thicken. Whisk in the oil very slowly at first, dripping it in off the tines of a fork, until about 2 tablespoons of oil has been incorporated. Switch to a hand-held beater, if preferred, and add more of the oil a little more quickly. Once the mixture is very thick, blend in 1 tablespoon of lemon juice then, whisking as you go, add the remaining oil in a thin steady stream. Taste and adjust seasoning, if required. If the mayonnaise tastes oily, add the rest of the lemon juice and some more salt. If the mayonnaise is too thick, thin it with cool, freshly boiled water. Add lemon pepper to taste. Cover the surface of the mayonnaise with plastic food wrap and keep chilled until serving time.

2 If using frozen calamari, thaw quickly in a sealed plastic bag in a basin of warm water. Rinse calamari rings and pat dry with paper towels. Cook on a preheated well oiled barbecue hot plate over medium heat for 1–2 minutes each side until a pale golden colour. Alternatively, heat 1 tablespoon of oil in a large ridged grill pan over medium heat. Add enough calamari to cover the base of the pan without crowding and cook rings for 1–2 minutes each side. Add more oil to the pan if necessary and reheat it before cooking more calamari. Transfer calamari to a bowl as they are cooked.

3 Toss garlic, parsley and rosemary through hot calamari. Season with a little sea salt and serve with mayonnaise.

avocados and prawns with lime and tomato salsa

SERVES 4
TIME TO PREP 25 MINUTES
TIME TO COOK 5 MINUTES

AVOCADOS, LIMES AND PRAWNS WITH A SPICY BITE SPELL SUMMER! THIS SALSA IS ALSO
GREAT ON TOAST – SIMPLY TOAST SLICES OF CIABATTA, SQUISH ON SOME AVOCADO AND
TOP WITH SALSA.

1 Prepare the salsa ingredients first. Plunge tomatoes into a saucepan of gently boiling water and count to ten, then use a slotted spoon to transfer tomatoes to a bowl of cold water. Peel the tomatoes; if they are hard to peel return them to the boiling water for a few more seconds. Quarter tomatoes, remove cores and flick out seeds. Dice flesh finely but don't add to salsa until just before serving.

2 Whisk together avocado or olive oil, lime juice, lime leaves, spring onion, chilli and salt.

3 If prawns are frozen, thaw them quickly in a sealed plastic bag immersed in a sink of warm water. Twist off their heads, then peel off shells, leaving the small piece of shell on the tail intact. Using a small sharp knife, slice down the back of each prawn and gently extract the red or black vein. Rinse prawns and pat dry with paper towels.

4 Put turmeric and cumin on a plate and rub spices over prawns. Halve avocados and remove the stones. Put avocado halves on serving plates. Cook prawns on a preheated oiled barbecue hot plate over medium heat for a few minutes each side until they change colour. Alternatively, cook prawns indoors in a hot ridged grill pan in 1 tablespoon of hot avocado or olive oil.

5 To serve, add tomatoes to salsa ingredients and spoon into the cavities of the avocados. Arrange prawns on top and serve immediately.

LIME AND TOMATO SALSA
2 medium-sized vine tomatoes
3 Tbsp extra virgin avocado or olive oil
1 Tbsp lime juice
4 kaffir lime leaves, centre ribs removed, finely shredded
1 spring onion (white and pale green part only), trimmed and finely chopped
1 fresh hot red chilli, halved, deseeded and finely chopped
½ tsp salt

12 medium-sized green (raw) prawns, fresh or frozen
¼ tsp ground turmeric
¼ tsp ground cumin
2 ripe but firm avocados
olive oil for hot plate

mini thai crab cakes

SERVES 8 (MAKES 30)
TIME TO PREP 30 MINUTES, PLUS 1 HOUR CHILLING
TIME TO COOK 10 MINUTES

CORIANDER ROOTS HAVE HEAPS OF FLAVOUR. IF THE CORIANDER YOU BUY HAS
ROOTS ATTACHED, TRIM AND WASH THEM AND STORE IN A PLASTIC BAG IN THE FREEZER
UNTIL REQUIRED.

CRAB CAKES

3 spring onions, trimmed and finely
  sliced
1–2 slim coriander roots, scrubbed
  and chopped, or 3 Tbsp chopped
  coriander leaves
2 fresh long red chillies, halved,
  deseeded and chopped
2 cloves garlic, peeled and crushed
1 Tbsp peeled and grated ginger
6 kaffir lime leaves, centre ribs
  removed, finely shredded, or
  finely grated zest of 2 limes
1 Tbsp fish sauce
250g firm white fish fillets, such as
  gurnard, finely chopped
250g fresh or canned crab meat,
  drained
75g bean-thread vermicelli noodles
1 small (size 5) free-range egg,
  lightly beaten
vegetable oil for hot plate

CHILLI DIPPING SAUCE
100ml white vinegar
1 fresh large hot red chilli, finely
  sliced
1 Tbsp fish sauce
1 spring onion, trimmed and
  finely sliced
1 Tbsp caster sugar

1 To make the crab cakes, put spring onions, coriander roots or coriander leaves, chillies, garlic, ginger, lime leaves or lime zest and fish sauce in a food processor fitted with the chopping blade. Process to a paste; you may need to scrape down the processor bowl once or twice. Transfer paste to a bowl and work in chopped fish and crab meat.

2 Put noodles in a bowl and pour over boiling water to cover. Soak for 5 minutes, drain, then snip noodles finely with scissors. Add noodles and egg to crab cake mixture. Blend well then shape into 30 small cakes. Refrigerate for at least one hour, but up to 6 hours, before cooking.

3 Cook crab cakes on a preheated well oiled barbecue hot plate over medium heat. Once the cakes are golden and crusty, turn carefully with 2 spoons and cook until golden on the other side. Spray or brush the hot plate with oil from time to time to keep them sizzling. Alternatively, fry crab cakes in hot oil in a frying pan until golden.

4 Meanwhile, in a small bowl mix dipping sauce ingredients together. Serve hot crab cakes with dipping sauce.

scallops with guacamole

SERVES 8 OR MORE (MAKES 24)
TIME TO PREP 20 MINUTES
TIME TO COOK 3 MINUTES

THESE SHOULD BE EATEN OR SLURPED STANDING UP, WITH A
GLASS OF CHAMPAGNE IN HAND. FOR NON-BUBBLY DRINKERS,
SAUVIGNON BLANC IS THE WAY TO GO.

2 medium-sized vine tomatoes
2 Tbsp finely chopped red onion
1 fresh hot red chilli, halved, deseeded and
    finely chopped
2 Tbsp chopped coriander leaves
1½ Tbsp lime juice
½ tsp salt
1½ Tbsp extra virgin avocado or olive oil
1 ripe but firm avocado
24 scallops (about 400g), trimmed and rinsed
1 Tbsp olive oil

1 Slice tomatoes into quarters, discard cores, and flick out
    seeds. Dice flesh finely then transfer to a sieve and drain
for 15 minutes.

2 Put red onion, chilli, coriander, lime juice, salt and
    avocado or olive oil in a bowl. Halve avocado, remove
stone and peel. Cut avocado flesh into tiny dice. Add to
bowl along with drained tomatoes.

3 Pat scallops dry with paper towels. Put them in a small
    bowl with 1 tablespoon of olive oil and toss until
coated. Cook scallops on a preheated barbecue hot plate
over medium heat for about 45 seconds each side, until
lightly browned and just cooked through. Alternatively, cook
scallops in a ridged grill pan heated until nice and hot and
cooked as described.

4 Gently toss guacamole mixture, then spoon a little of it
    on to small scallop shells or tiny dishes. Top each with a
hot plump scallop and devour!

prawn and chorizo bites

SERVES 6–8 (MAKES 20)
TIME TO PREP 15 MINUTES
TIME TO COOK 7 MINUTES

PRAWNS AND CHORIZO SAUSAGE MAY SEEM AN ODD
COMBINATION – MEAT AND SEAFOOD OFTEN IS – BUT THESE TWO
INGREDIENTS REALLY DO COMPLEMENT EACH OTHER.

20 large green (raw) prawns
2 soft chorizo sausages, thickly sliced
1 tsp smoked Spanish paprika (sweet)
1 Tbsp olive oil, plus extra for hot plate
finely grated zest of 2 lemons
20 short bamboo skewers, soaked in cold water
    for 30 minutes

1 If prawns are frozen, thaw them quickly in a sealed
    plastic bag immersed in a sink of warm water. Twist off
their heads, then peel off shells, leaving the small piece of
shell on the tail intact. Using a small sharp knife, slice down
the back of each prawn and gently extract the red or black
vein. Rinse prawns and pat dry with paper towels.

2 Spear 1 prawn and 1 slice of chorizo on each skewer;
    pierce the tail meat of each prawn first with the skewer
then curl the prawn in a spiral and pierce it again so that it
will keep a good shape as it cooks. Dust with a little paprika,
drizzle with oil and scatter with the zest of 1 lemon. (The
skewers can be prepared 1–2 hours ahead and refrigerated
until cooking time if preferred.)

3 Cook skewers on a preheated lightly oiled barbecue hot
    plate over medium heat until chorizo has coloured and
prawns are cooked through. Watch the lemon zest though
as it cooks quickly – remove pieces to a side plate once they
are golden. Alternatively, cook prawn and chorizo bites in
a little oil in a frying pan over medium heat. Serve hottish
scattered with the zest of the second lemon.

grilled aubergine rolls stuffed with feta

SERVES 6–8
TIME TO PREP 15 MINUTES
TIME TO COOK 20 MINUTES

THESE ARE A LITTLE MESSY TO EAT AS FINGER-FOOD, BUT THEY'RE SO GOOD THAT NOBODY MINDS THE DRIBBLES! SERVE THEM ON PLATES AS A STARTER, OR CUT THEM IN HALF OR INTO THIRDS TO SERVE WITH DRINKS.

1 Cut aubergines lengthways into thin slices. Put a little oil on a large plate and dunk several aubergine slices one at a time in the oil, letting excess oil drip off, then transfer them to a barbecue grill rack heated to medium. Cook quickly until tender and golden and lightly charred around the edges; you'll need to move the slices around often as they cook to prevent scorching. Transfer aubergine slices to a clean plate as they are done and season them with sea salt. Repeat with remaining aubergine slices. Alternatively, cook aubergine slices in a ridged grill pan over medium–high heat.

2 Put feta in a bowl. Chop mint or basil and add to feta along with lemon zest and 1 tablespoon of lemon juice. Spread a little of the feta over each slice of aubergine and roll up. Cut rolls in half. Arrange aubergine rolls on a platter. The aubergine rolls can be covered and kept at room temperature for 1–2 hours. If you want to prepare them well ahead, cover and refrigerate, but bring them to room temperature before serving.

3 Mix garlic, chilli, extra virgin olive oil, 1 tablespoon of lemon juice and a few pinches of sea salt in a small bowl. Spoon mixture over aubergine rolls and serve immediately.

2 large aubergines (eggplants)
olive oil
sea salt
200g creamy feta, mopped dry and crumbled
1 cup loosely packed, fresh mint or basil leaves
finely grated zest of 1 lemon
2 Tbsp lemon juice
2 cloves garlic, peeled and finely chopped
1 fresh hot red chilli, halved, deseeded and finely chopped
1 Tbsp extra virgin olive oil

Go to www.juliebiuso.com for a video clip of Julie demonstrating this recipe.

korean beef and lettuce cups

SERVES 6 OR MORE
TIME TO PREP 35 MINUTES, PLUS 30 MINUTES
   MARINATING
TIME TO COOK 5 MINUTES

THESE SPICY MORSELS ARE GREAT TO SHARE AROUND THE
BARBECUE WITH A CHILLED BEER.

small knob of fresh ginger, peeled
   and grated
1 clove garlic, peeled and crushed
3 spring onions, trimmed and finely sliced
½ tsp chilli paste
1 Tbsp caster sugar
2 Tbsp rice wine or dry sherry
3 Tbsp soy sauce
1 Tbsp sesame oil
1 Tbsp sweet chilli sauce, plus extra for serving
250g piece sirloin or 2 x 125g porterhouse steaks
olive oil for hot plate
1 cup jasmine rice, cooked
heart of an iceberg or buttercrunch lettuce, broken
   apart into cups, washed and dried
1 fresh hot red chilli, thinly sliced, for garnishing
1 Tbsp sesame seeds, lightly toasted in a dry pan
   for garnishing

1 Mix together ginger, garlic, spring onions, chilli paste,
sugar, rice wine or sherry, soy sauce, sesame oil and
sweet chilli sauce in a shallow dish. Trim beef then slice
thinly against the grain. Add to dish and toss well to coat the
beef. Cover and leave to marinate at room temperature for
30 minutes.

2 Drain beef but reserve the marinade. Cook beef over
high heat on a preheated oiled barbecue hot plate for a
few minutes until lightly browned. Transfer to a bowl. Boil
up marinade in a small saucepan and cook until thick and
syrupy. Pour juices over beef. Alternatively, heat a wok over
high heat and add the beef once it is nice and hot. Cook
beef quickly until lightly browned. Add marinade to wok and
cook as described.

3 To assemble beef and lettuce cups, put a small spoonful
of rice in each lettuce cup and top with a spoonful of
beef. Add a dollop of sweet chilli sauce, a sprinkling of
chopped red chilli and a smattering of sesame seeds to each
and serve immediately.

crispy bacon rolls with walnuts and tamarillo chutney

SERVES 6–8 (MAKES 24)
TIME TO PREP 12 MINUTES, PLUS 30 MINUTES TO SOAK
   THE PRUNES
TIME TO COOK 20 MINUTES

WHAT IS IT ABOUT BACON AND PRUNES THAT SENDS EVERYONE
INTO RAPTURES? THESE LITTLE DEVILS HAVE A TASTY SURPRISE OF
TAMARILLO CHUTNEY AND TOASTED WALNUTS HIDDEN INSIDE.

24 pitted prunes
¼ cup chopped walnuts
3–4 Tbsp tamarillo or peach chutney
12 rashers (about 250g) streaky bacon, halved
olive oil for hot plate

1 Soak prunes in freshly boiled water for 30 minutes. Drain
and dry off with paper towels.

2 Put walnuts in a shallow ovenproof dish and bake in an
oven preheated to 180°C for 7–10 minutes until golden.
Gently blow off any loose walnut skins.

3 Make a shallow cavity in each prune and put in half
a teaspoonful each of chopped walnuts and chutney.
Press prunes together to seal and wrap each one in a
piece of bacon. Cook bacon rolls on a preheated lightly
oiled barbecue hot plate over medium heat until golden.
Alternatively, cook bacon rolls under a preheated oven grill
until crisp, turning once or twice with tongs; you may need
to pour off accumulated juices that would burn off on a
barbecue. Cool for 5–7 minutes before serving.

sandwiches, snacks

Well-made crusty bread – the smell makes you go weak at the

knees – topped or stuffed with all manner of gorgeous titbits

to eat as a snack or as a substantial meal.

and stacks

best-ever steak and tomato sandwich with aïoli

SERVES 4
TIME TO PREP 20 MINUTES
TIME TO COOK 12 MINUTES

THIS IS A TASTY AND SATISFYING MEAL THAT MAKES STEAK GO A LITTLE FURTHER – YOU REALLY DON'T NEED MORE THAN ABOUT THREE-QUARTERS OF A STEAK PER SANDWICH.

AÏOLI
2 cloves garlic, peeled and finely crushed
3 medium (size 6) free-range egg yolks, at room temperature
½ tsp salt
300ml olive oil
2 Tbsp lemon juice

3 sirloin steaks, at room temperature
extra virgin olive oil
olive oil for hot plate
salt and freshly ground black pepper
3 large beefsteak tomatoes
finely grated zest of 1 lemon
caster sugar for sprinkling
8 slices sourdough bread
½ cup aïoli
½ cup tomato chutney
8 large leaves iceberg lettuce, shredded
8 gherkins, sliced
100g rocket, trimmed

1 To make the aïoli, whisk garlic, egg yolks and salt together in a small bowl until egg yolks darken and thicken. Drip in the oil a little at a time, beating continuously, until about one-third of the oil is added. Continue adding oil in a thin steady stream and beat continuously. Once the mayonnaise is very thick, add lemon juice and mix in, then continue adding the rest of the oil. Cover the surface with plastic food wrap. Refrigerate and use within 3 days.

2 Rub steaks with oil and grind over plenty of black pepper. Cook on a preheated oiled barbecue hot plate over high heat until done to your liking; be careful not to overcook the steaks. Alternatively, cook steaks in a ridged grill pan over medium–high heat. Transfer to a plate and season liberally with salt. Rest steaks for 10 minutes before slicing; discard fat as you slice the meat.

3 Slice tomatoes thickly, sprinkle them with lemon zest and caster sugar and cook on an oiled barbecue hot plate until golden on one side only. Transfer to a plate as they are done. Lightly char the slices of bread on a preheated barbecue grill rack over gentle heat; take care as the bread burns easily. Alternatively, cook it under a preheated oven grill, or in a ridged frying pan. Put 4 slices of the bread on plates and spread with a little aïoli and chutney. Stack with iceberg lettuce, gherkins, tomatoes and a few dollops of aïoli. Season with salt and pepper, then top with slices of steak and rocket. Spread the remaining slices of toasted sourdough with remaining aïoli and chutney and put on top of the sandwiches. Serve hot.

bruschetta with beetroot, goat's cheese and toasted walnuts

SERVES 4–8 AS A STARTER (MAKES 8 SLICES)
TIME TO PREP 15 MINUTES
TIME TO COOK 1 HOUR

POMEGRANATE MOLASSES IS TANGY-SWEET AND WORKS WELL HERE WITH SWEET BEETROOT
AND GOAT'S CHEESE, BUT YOU COULD USE BALSAMIC VINEGAR INSTEAD.

1 Wash beetroot. Trim the leaves and tapering roots if they are very long, but don't nick the skin or beetroot flesh or the beetroot will bleed during cooking. Put beetroot in a saucepan and cover generously with cold water. Bring to the boil, lower the heat and cook gently for about 45 minutes until tender. Drain beetroot and refresh with cold water. When cool enough to touch, slip off skins and discard any attached roots and leaves; I like to wear disposable food gloves to do this to avoid staining my hands.

2 Cut each beetroot into thick slices. Toss beetroot with 1 tablespoon of walnut oil, lemon juice, a few pinches of salt and freshly ground black pepper to taste.

3 Toast walnut halves for 7–10 minutes in an oven preheated to 180°C. Pick off excess walnut skin with a clean toothpick and gently blow off loose skins. Chop coarsely.

4 Lightly char the slices of bread on a preheated barbecue grill rack over gentle heat; take care as the bread burns easily. Alternatively, cook it under an oven grill, or in a ridged frying pan. Rub each slice on one side with a cut clove of garlic. Drizzle with a little extra virgin olive oil and sprinkle with sea salt. Stack with watercress or rocket, beetroot and goat's cheese, then drizzle with a little walnut oil and a good dousing of pomegranate molasses. Garnish with chopped toasted walnut halves and serve immediately.

250g small beetroot
walnut oil, plus extra for serving
1 Tbsp lemon juice
salt and freshly ground black pepper
8 fresh walnut halves for garnishing
8 slices ciabatta
1 large clove garlic, peeled and halved
extra virgin olive oil
sea salt
120g watercress or rocket, trimmed
100g soft tangy goat's cheese, sliced into 8 rounds
3 Tbsp pomegranate molasses

grilled chicken sandwiches with rouille and roasted tomatoes

SERVES 6
TIME TO PREP 40 MINUTES
TIME TO COOK 30 MINUTES

ROASTED TOMATOES

6 medium–large vine tomatoes, halved
caster sugar
sea salt and freshly ground black pepper
lemon-infused extra virgin olive oil
12 large mint leaves

ROUILLE

large pinch saffron threads
3 cloves garlic, peeled and split in half
1 tsp salt
1 slice ciabatta bread, crusts removed (crustless slice should weigh about 30g)
¼ tsp smoked Spanish paprika (sweet)
2 Tbsp tomato juice
2 large (size 7) free-range egg yolks, at room temperature
1 Tbsp creamy Dijonnaise mustard
1 cup olive oil
2 Tbsp lemon juice
1 small red pepper (capsicum), roasted and finely diced (see page 30)
1 Tbsp chopped flat-leaf parsley

SANDWICHES

1 small red onion, peeled and cut into fine slivers
600g free-range chicken schnitzels or 6 thin slices free-range, skinned chicken breast
olive oil
salt and freshly ground black pepper
6 slices ciabatta bread
2–3 cups baby salad greens or cos lettuce leaves, torn

THIS IS A FEISTY SNACK – HOT, SHARP AND SPICY. ALLOW PLENTY OF TIME TO MAKE ALL THE COMPONENTS. IT'S GREAT WITH A CHILLED BEER.

1 To roast tomatoes, put them cut side up in a shallow tin, such as a Swiss roll tin, lined with baking paper. Sprinkle with a little sugar and a little sea salt, grind over some pepper and drizzle with a little oil. Put a mint leaf on each tomato half. Bake in an oven preheated to 225°C (fanbake) for 15–20 minutes until tomatoes start charring around the edges and losing shape.

2 To make the rouille, toast saffron strands in a small dry frying pan over a gentle heat for a few minutes. Roughly chop garlic then crush it with the saffron and half a teaspoon of salt in a mortar and pestle. Add bread, pound to break up the bread, then add the smoked paprika and tomato juice and pound to a purée. Whisk egg yolks, mustard and remaining salt in a bowl. Drip in the oil off the tines of a fork. Once half a cup of the oil is whisked in, the mixture should be nice and thick. Blend in 1 tablespoon of lemon juice, then start adding remaining oil a little more quickly, in a thin even stream. Blend in the last tablespoon of lemon juice, then the pounded bread mixture, roasted and finely diced red pepper and parsley.

3 To prepare the sandwich fillings, first soak red onion in a bowl of icy cold water until ready to assemble, then drain and pat dry.

4 Toss chicken in a shallow dish with 1 tablespoon oil and plenty of ground black pepper. Cook chicken schnitzels on a preheated oiled barbecue hot plate over medium heat until the chicken is about 75% white, then flip over and cook the other side for a few minutes, until just cooked through. Transfer chicken to a plate and season with salt. Alternatively, heat a ridged grill pan over medium heat. Once it's hot, put in several pieces of chicken. Cook for 3–5 minutes until the chicken no longer sticks to the pan, and it is a good golden brown. Turn chicken over and continue cooking until just cooked through. Repeat with the remaining chicken pieces.

5 To assemble the sandwiches, first lightly char the slices of bread on both sides on a preheated barbecue grill rack over gentle heat; take care as the bread burns easily. Alternatively, cook it under a preheated oven grill, or in a ridged grill pan. Put the toasted ciabatta on a large plate or 6 individual plates and stack with salad greens, rouille, chicken, slivered onions and roasted tomatoes and serve immediately.

portobello mushrooms with prosciutto and balsamic vinegar

SERVES 6 AS A STARTER OR SNACK
TIME TO PREP 12 MINUTES
TIME TO COOK 15 MINUTES

I LIKE THESE MUSHROOMS ON ROBUST BREAD BECAUSE THE JUICES MAKE SOFT BREAD GO SOGGY.

30g butter
2 cloves garlic, peeled and crushed
½ Tbsp chopped rosemary
12 flat portobello mushrooms
salt and freshly ground black pepper
60g mesclun salad mix or baby salad leaves
extra virgin olive oil
6 thin slices grainy or sourdough bread, toasted on the grill
6 thin slices prosciutto
balsamic vinegar

1 Put butter in a bowl with garlic and rosemary and melt in a microwave. Alternatively, put the bowl in a sink of very hot water and stir until melted.

2 Wipe mushrooms clean with a damp cloth. Brush them all over with melted garlic and rosemary butter. Sprinkle with a little salt and grind on some pepper. Cook mushrooms on a preheated barbecue hot plate over low–medium heat until tender and browned. Alternatively, put them in one layer in a shallow ovenproof dish lined with baking paper with the stalks pointing up. Bake them in an oven preheated to 200°C for about 15 minutes until tender and crispy around the edges. Transfer mushrooms to a plate and let them cool for 5 minutes.

3 While the mushrooms are cooling, dress the salad greens with a little extra virgin olive oil, salt and pepper. Put the toast on plates; if sourdough slices are large, cut them in half and put two pieces on each plate. Pile the dressed greens on the bread, then put two mushrooms on top of each pile of greens and arrange curls of prosciutto on top. Drizzle with a little balsamic vinegar and serve immediately.

mozzarella and chargrilled aubergine stack

SERVES 4 AS A SUBSTANTIAL SNACK OR LIGHT MEAL
  (MAKES 8)
TIME TO PREP 15 MINUTES
TIME TO COOK 15 MINUTES

AUBERGINE THAT IS NOT COOKED PROPERLY MAKES YOUR
MOUTH GO FURRY – IT'S REALLY UNPLEASANT! CUT IT INTO THIN
SLICES ABOUT 1.5 CENTIMETRES THICK AND COOK UNTIL IT'S A
GOOD DEEP BROWN. COOKING THEM OVER A BARBECUE GRILL
RACK MEANS YOU WILL USE LESS OIL AND KEEP THE MESS OUT OF
YOUR KITCHEN.

1 large firm aubergine (eggplant)
olive oil
sea salt and freshly ground black pepper
200g buffalo mozzarella, drained and mopped dry
300g loaf of ciabatta bread
2 Tbsp capers, drained
¼ cup mint leaves
¼ cup basil leaves
extra virgin olive oil
lemon wedges or balsamic vinegar for serving

1 Cut aubergine lengthways into thin slices. Put a little olive oil on a large plate and dunk slices one at a time in the oil, letting excess oil drip off. Transfer aubergine to a barbecue grill rack heated to medium. You'll need to move the slices around often as they cook to prevent scorching. Cook quickly until tender, golden and lightly charred around the edges. Transfer aubergine slices to a clean plate as they are done and season with sea salt. Repeat with remaining aubergine slices. Alternatively, cook aubergine slices in a ridged frying pan over medium–high heat. Cut each slice into 3–4 pieces when cool.

2 Slice mozzarella into 2–3cm thick slices. Cut ciabatta lengthways down the centre to make two long halves, then cut each piece into four. Put ciabatta slices on an oven tray, crust-side up, and toast under a grill until golden. Turn slices over and top with sliced mozzarella; you may need to mop the cheese again if it has thrown off a lot of moisture while standing. Return ciabatta to the grill and cook until cheese is bubbling and slightly golden.

3 Arrange ciabatta slices on a platter and divide the aubergine among them. Scatter with capers, mint and basil leaves, season everything with a little sea salt and freshly ground black pepper and drizzle with a little extra virgin olive oil. Serve with lemon wedges or splash with balsamic vinegar before serving.

bacon and egg butties

SERVES 4
TIME TO PREP 12 MINUTES
TIME TO COOK 12 MINUTES

IF YOUR KIDS LOVE BACON AND EGGS, ADD GOODNESS BY USING
WHOLEGRAIN BREAD AND INCLUDING AVOCADO, TOMATO,
PARSLEY AND LETTUCE. THERE IS A SKILL TO COOKING EGGS ON
A BARBECUE PLATE – IF YOU'RE NOT CAREFUL THEY'LL RUN OFF
THE SLIPPERY PLATE AND DISAPPEAR INTO THE DRIP TRAY! USE
BARBECUE SCRAPERS OR TOOLS TO HOLD THEM IN PLACE FOR
A FEW SECONDS UNTIL THE EGG WHITE STARTS TO SET, THEN
THEY'LL STAY PUT. BREAKING EGGS INTO A JUG MAKES IT EASIER
TO POUR THEM.

8 rashers streaky free-range bacon
olive oil for hot plate
4 medium (size 6) free-range eggs
salt and freshly ground black pepper
1 ripe but firm avocado
lemon juice
4 large wholegrain bread rolls
1–2 large beefsteak tomatoes, sliced and drained
iceberg lettuce leaves
2 Tbsp chopped parsley

1 Cook bacon on a preheated oiled barbecue hot plate over medium–low heat until crisp. Alternatively, cook it under a grill, or fry in a little hot oil in a frying pan. Transfer to a plate lined with paper towels to mop up excess fat.

2 Break eggs into a jug one at a time, keeping yolks whole. Gently pour each egg onto the oiled barbecue

hot plate and cook until done to your liking. Season eggs with salt and pepper. Alternatively, fry eggs in an oiled non-stick frying pan.

3 Halve avocado, remove stone and peel. Slice thickly and sprinkle over a little lemon juice. Toast the rolls, put the eggs on the bases and stack with bacon, avocado, tomato and lettuce and, finally, parsley. Put lids on rolls and serve immediately.

isanna's eggs on ciabatta

SERVES 4 AS A SUBSTANTIAL SNACK OR LIGHT MEAL
  (MAKES 12)
TIME TO PREP 20 MINUTES
TIME TO COOK 10 MINUTES

ISANNA, MY ITALIAN SISTER-IN-LAW, GREW UP CLOSE TO REGGIO EMILIA IN ITALY WITH HOME-RAISED CHICKENS AND RABBITS, HOMEGROWN FRUIT AND VEGETABLES, PLUS ALL THE GLORIES OF THE REGION – PROSCIUTTO, PARMIGIANO, MORTADELLA, BALSAMICO. I'M NOT JEALOUS, OF COURSE – NOT AT ALL! I'VE ADAPTED THIS SALAD OF HERS TO GO ON BRUSCHETTA, AND IT'S REALLY SCRUMPTIOUS. SERVE WITH A GREEN SALAD.

6 large (size 7) free-range eggs, at room temperature
12 slices ciabatta bread
½ cup kalamata olives, drained, pitted and chopped
3 cloves garlic, peeled and finely chopped
3 Tbsp coarsely chopped flat-leaf parsley
freshly ground black pepper
sea salt
freshly pressed extra virgin olive oil for drizzling
3–4 thin slices prosciutto or Serrano ham

1 Prick the rounded ends of the eggs with a pin. Carefully lower eggs into a pan of gently boiling water and cook gently for 7 minutes. Drain off the hot water, then run cold water over eggs for several minutes. Peel eggs as soon as they are cool to touch. Cut eggs in half and discard 2 egg

whites (they're not required in this mix) then finely chop remaining whites with the yolks.

2 Lightly char the slices of bread over the barbecue grill rack; take care as the bread burns easily. Alternatively, cook it under an oven grill, or in a ridged grill pan. Transfer to plates as they are done and spread with chopped egg. Scatter chopped olives and garlic over the egg; use two teaspoons to do this or the garlic will stick to your fingers. Top with a smattering of parsley. Grind on a little black pepper, sprinkle on a little sea salt and drizzle generously with oil.

3 Arrange curls of prosciutto or ham on top of each piece and serve immediately. This is best eaten with knives and forks.

bruschetta with asparagus and prosciutto

MAKES 10 SLICES
TIME TO PREP 20 MINUTES
TIME TO COOK 12 MINUTES

THERE'S SOMETHING ABOUT GARLIC, ROSEMARY AND WHITE BEANS THAT IS UTTERLY, UTTERLY DELICIOUS. IF YOU'VE NEVER EATEN THEM TOGETHER, THIS SIMPLE BEAN PURÉE WILL BE A REVELATION. SERVE THIS AS A LUXURIOUS SNACK WITH DRINKS, OR TO A SMALLER GROUP FOR A LIGHT MEAL.

BEAN PURÉE
2 Tbsp extra virgin olive oil
1 large clove garlic, peeled and crushed
1 Tbsp finely chopped rosemary
3 tiny dried bird's eye chillies, crushed
1 x 425g can cannellini beans, drained, rinsed and drained
¼ tsp salt

BRUSCHETTA AND TOPPING
20 asparagus spears
finely grated zest of 1 lemon
extra virgin olive oil
salt and freshly ground black pepper
olive oil for hot plate
10 thickish slices ciabatta bread
2 fat cloves garlic, peeled and halved
10 thin slices prosciutto

1 To make the bean purée, heat the oil in a small frying pan over medium heat and add the garlic, rosemary and crushed chillies. Sauté for 2–3 minutes and mix in the beans and salt. Transfer to a food processor and blend to a purée; if the purée is very stiff, thin with a little warm water. (If making a day ahead, cool, cover and refrigerate, but serve at room temperature.)

2 To prepare the topping, snap woody ends off the asparagus spears or trim them with a knife. Wash asparagus under running water and pat dry. Mix lemon zest with 2 tablespoons of oil in a large shallow dish with a few pinches of salt and plenty of black pepper. Add asparagus spears and roll them around the dish to coat. Cook asparagus spears on a preheated oiled barbecue hot plate over medium heat for about 10 minutes, turning often, until golden brown. Remove lemon zest to a side plate as it browns.

3 Lightly char the slices of bread on both sides on a preheated barbecue grill rack over gentle heat; take care as the bread burns easily. Alternatively, cook it under an oven grill, or in a ridged grill pan. Rub each slice on one side with a cut clove of garlic. Spread with warm bean purée and top with barbecued asparagus spears and curls of prosciutto. Serve immediately. Alternatively, if the weather is foul, cook the bread under the oven grill or simply pop it in a toaster and cook the asparagus in a shallow tin, such as a Swiss roll tin, lined with baking paper in a preheated oven (180°C) until golden.

smoked fish, avocado and orange on bruschetta

SERVES 6 AS A SUBSTANTIAL SNACK OR LIGHT MEAL (MAKES 12 SLICES)
TIME TO PREP 25 MINUTES
TIME TO COOK 5 MINUTES

FISH IS SMOKED TO PRESERVE IT, BUT HERE'S THE RUB – IT'S AT ITS MOST JUICY, SUCCULENT
BEST IMMEDIATELY AFTER SMOKING, AND DRIES A LITTLE MORE AS EACH DAY GOES BY. I
FIND OUT WHEN MY LOCAL FISHMONGER IS SMOKING FISH, AND THAT'S THE DAY I BUY IT
AND USE IT – WHILE IT'S STILL WARM FROM THE SMOKER.

1 Remove skin and bones from fish then flake the flesh. Put fish in a covered container and refrigerate until 5 minutes before assembling bruschetta.

2 Slice onion very thinly and soak in a bowl of icy cold water for 15 minutes. Drain and dry on paper towels.

3 Peel oranges with a small serrated knife, then cut in between each piece of membrane and let the orange segments fall into a bowl. Squeeze any juice in the membrane over the orange pieces.

4 Roughly chop green olives and put in a small bowl with garlic, chilli, parsley, extra virgin olive oil and 2 tablespoons of orange juice taken from the bowl of orange segments. Stir together.

5 Lightly char the slices of bread on one side over the barbecue grill rack; take care as the bread burns easily. Alternatively, cook it under an oven grill, or in a ridged frying pan. Halve avocados, remove stones and scoop out flesh. Spread avocado over the ciabatta on the untoasted side or slice avocado into thick slices and arrange on ciabatta. Season avocado with salt and squirt on a little lemon juice. Top with smoked fish and garnish with orange segments and red onion. Spoon over olive salsa and serve immediately.

1 medium-sized smoked fish (600–700g) or 2 cups (350g) flaked, smoked fish
1 small red onion, peeled
2 juicy oranges
¾ cup pimiento-stuffed green olives, drained
2 cloves garlic, peeled and finely chopped
1 fresh hot green chilli, finely chopped
3 Tbsp coarsely chopped flat-leaf parsley
3 Tbsp extra virgin olive oil
12 slices ciabatta bread
2 large ripe but firm avocados
salt
½ a lemon

bruschetta with spanish beans, broad beans and sizzled ham

SERVES 4–6 AS A LIGHT MEAL (MAKES 12)
TIME TO PREP 25 MINUTES
TIME TO COOK 10 MINUTES

THIS IS IMPRESSIVE – AND HOW COULD IT NOT BE, WITH THE MARRIAGE OF BEANS AND THE SHARP CLEAN BITE OF SHERRY VINEGAR CUTTING THROUGH SWEET CARAMELISED HAM.

400g fresh broad beans or 200g frozen broad beans
3 Tbsp butter
salt and freshly ground black pepper
250g (2 thick slices) ham off the bone, cut into large chunks
600g cooked white beans, canned or bottled, drained, rinsed and drained
300g loaf ciabatta bread
3 Tbsp sherry vinegar or white wine vinegar
¼ cup mint leaves

1 If the broad beans are fresh, remove them from their pods and drop them into a saucepan of lightly salted boiling water. Return to the boil and cook for 10 minutes, or until tender. Drain and refresh with cold water. If using frozen broad beans, cook in the same manner, but for 3 minutes only once the water returns to the boil. Next, remove the beans from their skins (fiddly but necessary). Put beans in a saucepan with a dot of butter, season with salt and pepper and set aside.

2 Heat a large frying pan over medium heat and, when it is hot, drop in a large tablespoon of butter. Once it sizzles add the ham and cook until golden on both sides. Transfer to a plate. Add a second tablespoon of butter to the pan and add the white beans. Squash them with a fork, turning them into a coarse purée. Season with a little salt and pepper.

3 Cut ciabatta lengthways through the centre to make 2 long pieces, then cut each piece into six. Lightly char the pieces of bread over a preheated barbecue grill rack; take care as the bread burns easily. Alternatively, cook under an oven grill, or in a ridged frying pan. Spread with white bean purée and top with sizzled ham. Gently heat broad beans in a saucepan then spoon over the ham.

4 Add vinegar to the frying pan which had the white bean purée in it and heat gently. Stir the vinegar in the pan, scraping the base to lift up any sediment or crusty bits of bean purée. Stir in the remaining butter. Remove pan from heat and spoon juices over the bruschetta. Scatter with mint, grind over black pepper to taste and serve immediately.

grilled pizza

MAKES 4
TIME TO PREP 20 MINUTES
TIME TO COOK 40 MINUTES

PIZZA ON THE BARBECUE – IF YOU DON'T HAVE A PIZZA OVEN, THIS IS THE WAY TO GO. YOU'LL GET A CRISPIER BASE BROWNING IT ON THE BARBECUE GRILL THAN COOKING IT IN THE OVEN. IF YOU WANT TO MAKE MEATLESS PIZZAS, SUBSTITUTE GRILLED ARTICHOKES FOR THE CHORIZO OR SAUSAGES.

TOMATO SAUCE
2 Tbsp olive oil
2 cloves garlic, peeled and crushed
1 x 400g can Italian tomatoes, crushed
salt and freshly ground black pepper

PIZZA
3 fresh chorizo sausages or 3–4 small free-range pork
  and fennel-seed flavoured sausages or 1 x 400g jar
  grilled artichoke hearts in oil
olive oil
4 uncooked pizza bases
extra virgin olive oil
coarse semolina or polenta
½ cup shaved parmesan cheese
1 cup basil leaves
250g buffalo or cow's milk mozzarella, drained
  and mopped dry
salt and freshly ground black pepper
handful of rocket leaves, trimmed
small wedge of parmesan cheese for shaving

Go to www.juliebiuso.com for a video clip of Julie demonstrating this recipe.

1 Make the sauce first. Put the oil and garlic in a small saucepan over medium heat. Let garlic take on a little colour, then add the tomatoes. Bring to a gentle boil, season with ¼ teaspoon salt and a little pepper, then lower the heat and cook gently for 10 minutes.

2 If making meat pizzas, slice chorizo or sausages and fry in a little hot oil. If using artichokes, drain well, mop with paper towels and slice thinly.

3 Brush one side of the pizza bases with extra virgin olive oil. Cook over a preheated barbecue grill rack over low–medium heat for 4–5 minutes until lightly charred; put the bases straight on the rack. Transfer to a baking sheet using tongs. Brown all the bases before cooking the first pizza.

4 Assemble one pizza at a time and while it is cooking, assemble the next one. Flip pizza base over onto a piece of baking paper or a pizza peel sprinkled with coarse semolina or polenta to prevent sticking so that the grilled side is facing up. Scatter pizza with a little cheese, then put on dollops of tomato sauce. Arrange cooked meat or sliced artichokes on top, then basil and mozzarella. Season with a little salt and pepper.

5 Slide pizza back onto the hot barbecue grill rack and cook for about 5 minutes, until the underside is nicely browned. Transfer pizza to a baking sheet and brown the top under a hot grill, cooking until cheese is melted. Alternatively, if you are cooking on a hooded barbecue, cook the assembled pizza with the hood down. The heat probably won't be sufficient to brown the cheese, but it will melt it.

6 Strew a little rocket over the top of the cooked pizza and add a few shavings of parmesan cheese and serve immediately.

gourmet beef burgers

MAKES 4
TIME TO PREP 25 MINUTES, PLUS 30 MINUTES CHILLING
TIME TO COOK 15 MINUTES

HAMBURGERS WITH ALL THE TRIMMINGS ARE ALWAYS POPULAR. TOP THESE TASTY BURGERS WITH CARAMELISED ONIONS AND WATCH THEM DISAPPEAR. BUY MINCE THE DAY YOU INTEND TO USE IT AS IT IS NOT AS LONG-KEEPING AS SLICED MEAT OR LARGER CUTS OF MEAT.

BEEF PATTIES
4 Tbsp ready-made tomato sauce
1 small onion, peeled and finely chopped

1 large clove garlic, peeled and crushed
1 Tbsp chopped rosemary
salt and freshly ground black pepper
1 medium (size 6) free-range egg, lightly beaten
500g minced beef
½ cup fresh white breadcrumbs

BURGERS
4 medium-sized red onions, peeled and thickly sliced
olive oil for hot plate
4 soft baps or hamburger buns
butter or mayonnaise
4 large iceberg lettuce leaves, torn into
   bite-sized pieces
1 large tomato, sliced
4 gherkins, sliced
ready-made tomato sauce
½ cup grated tasty cheese

1 To make the patties, put all the ingredients in a large bowl and squelch together. Shape meat into 4 patties slightly larger then the baps or buns you have chosen. I wear disposable food gloves to do this. Alternatively, make 6 or 8 thinner patties and provide more baps or buns and filling.

2 Stack patties in a container, separating each with a double thickness of waxed paper or plastic food wrap, and chill for 30 minutes or until ready to cook. Bring patties to room temperature about 15 minutes before cooking.

3 To assemble burgers, first cook onions very gently on a well oiled barbecue hot plate until golden brown, stirring often; this will take about 15 minutes. Alternatively, cook them in 3 tablespoons of oil in a large frying pan over medium–high heat. Prepare remaining ingredients.

4 Cook patties on a preheated oiled barbecue hot plate over medium heat until nicely coloured. Flip patties over and lower the heat a little and cook gently until cooked all the way through. Alternatively, heat 2 tablespoons oil in a frying pan over medium heat, and when hot, slip patties into pan. Cook for about 5 minutes, until well browned, flip over and cook second side.

5 Toast baps or buns and spread with butter or mayonnaise. Stack the bases with lettuce, patties, a few slices of tomato and gherkin and dribble on a little tomato sauce. Scatter cheese over and spoon on caramelised onions. Place lids on top and serve immediately.

bruschetta with guacamole and crispy bacon

SERVES 4 AS A LIGHT MEAL (MAKES 12)
TIME TO PREP 20 MINUTES
TIME TO COOK 10 MINUTES

THESE CAN ALSO BE SERVED AS A PRE-BARBECUE SNACK.

2 ripe but firm avocados
1 Tbsp lime juice
½ tsp sea salt
2 fresh hot red chillies, finely chopped (remove seeds
   for a milder flavour)
2 spring onions, trimmed and finely chopped (white
   and pale green part only)
2 Tbsp chopped coriander leaves
12 thick slices ciabatta bread
2 fat cloves garlic, peeled and halved
avocado oil
12 rashers streaky bacon
olive oil for hot plate
¼ cup sour cream
½ cup kalamata olives, pitted and chopped

1 Halve avocados, remove stones and scoop out flesh. Mash with lime juice and sea salt, then mix in chillies, spring onions and coriander. Cover the surface of the guacamole with plastic food wrap and chill until ready to serve.

2 Lightly char the slices of bread on both sides on a preheated barbecue grill rack over gentle heat; take care as the bread burns easily. Alternatively, cook it under a preheated oven grill, or in a ridged grill pan. Rub each slice on one side with a cut clove of garlic. Arrange bruschetta on a large platter and drizzle with a little avocado oil.

3 Cook bacon on a lightly oiled preheated barbecue hot plate over medium heat until crisp. Alternatively, cook bacon under a preheated oven grill or fry in a little hot oil in a frying pan. Pat with paper towels to absorb excess fat. Stack bruschetta with guacamole, dollops of sour cream, a sprinkle of chopped olives and, finally, the rashers of crispy bacon. Serve immediately.

lamburgers with middle-eastern flavours

SERVES 6
TIME TO PREP 20 MINUTES, PLUS 30 MINUTES CHILLING
TIME TO COOK 7–10 MINUTES

THIS YOGHURT AND TAHINI SAUCE, WITH ITS FRESH SCENT OF MINT AND EARTHY TONES OF CUMIN, REALLY MAKES THESE LAMBURGERS SPECIAL. YOU COULD ADD A DOLLOP OR TWO OF RELISH TO SPICE THINGS UP AND SLICES OF TOMATOES, GHERKINS AND BEETROOT, IF LIKED. THE SAUCE IS ALSO GREAT WITH GRILLED LAMB CUTLETS, CHICKEN BREASTS AND WHOLE BARBECUED FISH.

LAMB PATTIES
750g minced lamb
2 medium (size 6) free-range egg yolks
¼ tsp allspice
¼ tsp ground cinnamon
2 cloves garlic, peeled and crushed
1 tsp salt
2 Tbsp water
1 Tbsp pomegranate molasses, optional

YOGHURT SAUCE
1 cup plain yoghurt
3 Tbsp tahini
2 Tbsp chopped mint
½ tsp ground cumin
pinch of salt

olive oil for hot plate
6 baps or panini, toasted and split, for serving
iceberg lettuce leaves for serving

1 To make the patties, put all the ingredients in a large bowl and squelch together; I wear disposable food gloves to do this. Shape into 6 patties slightly larger than the baps or panini you have chosen. Put patties on a plate, cover with plastic food wrap and chill for 30 minutes. Bring patties to room temperature about 15 minutes before cooking.

2 To make the sauce, mix ingredients together in a small bowl and set aside.

3 Cook patties on a preheated lightly oiled barbecue hot plate over low–medium heat, letting them sizzle along nicely without charring; mince must be cooked all the way through, so don't hurry the job or you'll end up with charred patties that are still raw in the middle. Press down on the patties with a spatula once or twice during cooking. You shouldn't need any extra oil because lamb mince will ooze fat as it cooks. Alternatively, fry patties in a little oil in a ridged grill pan.

4 To assemble burgers, place the toasted bap or panini bases on a plate and stack with lettuce, patties, yoghurt sauce and optional extras, if using. Serve immediately.

things on sticks

Tasty morsels of food speared on bamboo sticks, rosemary stalks,

lemon grass stems or lollipop sticks and cooked over the grill until

sizzling, fragrant and utterly irresistible.

chicken lollipops

SERVES 4–6 (MAKES 24)
TIME TO PREP 20 MINUTES, PLUS 2 HOURS CHILLING
TIME TO COOK 10 MINUTES

FAST, FABULOUS AND FUN – THESE CHICKEN STICKS ARE LIKED BY EVERYONE. I LIKE
THEM WITH A REAL KICK, BUT FOR A MILDER FLAVOUR USE LESS CHILLI. THEY'RE GREAT
WITH PEANUT SAUCE OR YOGHURT AND MINT.

750g free-range chicken mince
1 free-range egg yolk
¾ tsp salt
2 cloves garlic, peeled and crushed
1 Tbsp peeled and grated ginger
1 Tbsp coarsely ground coriander
   seeds
finely grated zest of 1 lime
1 fresh hot red chilli, finely chopped
   (remove seeds for a milder
   flavour)
olive oil for hot plate
sea salt
lime wedges or soy sauce for
   serving

ice-cream sticks (available from
   supermarkets)

1 Mix chicken mince, egg yolk and salt together in a large bowl. Add garlic, ginger, coriander seeds, lime zest and chilli and squelch together; I wear disposable food gloves to do this. Shape into elongated patties and press onto ice-cream sticks. Put the 'lollipops' on a plate as they are done and chill for 2 hours.

2 Cook patties on a preheated oiled barbecue hot plate over medium heat until golden brown all over; keep patties lightly oiled during cooking to prevent them becoming dry. Don't leave the patties unattended or they will char. Turn them often to achieve an even golden brown. Alternatively, cook them in a little hot oil in a ridged grill pan over medium heat.

3 Sprinkle with sea salt and serve hot, with lime wedges for squeezing over or soy sauce for dipping.

beef satay

SERVES 6–8 (MAKES ABOUT 24 SKEWERS)
TIME TO PREP 20 MINUTES, PLUS AT LEAST 1 HOUR MARINATING
TIME TO COOK 5 MINUTES

SATAY IS A QUINTESSENTIAL MALAY DISH. FOR AN AUTHENTIC FLAVOUR, KEEP THE MEAT THINLY SLICED OR CUT INTO SMALL CUBES, AND COOK THE SATAY QUICKLY OVER HOT COALS. BRUSH SATAY WITH A SMASHED STEM OF LEMON GRASS DIPPED IN OIL DURING COOKING FOR ADDED FLAVOUR. SERVE CHUNKS OF RED ONION AND CUCUMBER, LEMON WEDGES AND SPICY SATAY SAUCE (SEE PAGE 144) ON THE SIDE.

850g rump or sirloin steak
1 tsp brown sugar
2 cloves garlic, peeled and crushed
1½ Tbsp crushed coriander seeds
1 tsp ground chilli paste
2 stalks lemon grass, smashed
olive oil

24 bamboo skewers, soaked in cold water for 30 minutes

1 Trim steak, then slice into very thin strips down the length of the steak, cutting against the grain of the meat. Transfer to a bowl and mix in sugar, garlic, coriander seeds, chilli and 1 stalk of lemon grass with your hands; wear disposable food gloves when handling chillies. Cover and marinate in the refrigerator for 1–24 hours.

2 Thread meat onto skewers. Cook satay over hot coals for 2–3 minutes a side, brushing with oil with the remaining stalk of lemon grass, until browned; don't overcook – the meat is thin and cooks quickly. Let the satay flare just a little towards the end of cooking to take on a hint of smoke. Alternatively, cook on a preheated barbecue grill rack over medium heat or on an oiled barbecue hot plate or in a non-stick frying pan over medium heat. Arrange on a platter or individual plates and serve immediately.

pork satay

SERVES 6–8 (MAKES 20–24 SKEWERS)
TIME TO PREP 20 MINUTES, PLUS 15 MINUTES MARINATING
TIME TO COOK 5 MINUTES

A GOOD STANDARD PORK SATAY, THIS DOESN'T NEED A LONG TIME TO MARINATE. IT DOES HAVE A BIT OF BITE, SO SERVE IT WITH COOLING CHUNKS OF SLICED CUCUMBER, MINT LEAVES AND TORN ICEBERG LETTUCE ON THE SIDE.

600g free-range pork fillet
1½ Tbsp lime juice
4 kaffir lime leaves, centre ribs
   removed, finely shredded
1½ Tbsp brown sugar
2 Tbsp fish sauce
2 Tbsp coarsely grated ginger
3 cloves garlic, peeled and chopped
1 fresh hot red chilli, finely chopped
2 stalks lemon grass, smashed with
   a mallet
olive oil

24 bamboo skewers, soaked in cold
   water for 30 minutes

DIPPING SAUCE
2 Tbsp lime juice
1 tsp sugar
1½ Tbsp fish sauce
1 fresh hot red chilli, thinly sliced
1 Tbsp torn coriander sprigs

1 Using a small sharp knife, remove silverskin from pork fillet then cut meat into small cubes. Mix lime juice, lime leaves, sugar, fish sauce, ginger, garlic, chilli and lemon grass in a shallow dish and stir through pork cubes. Marinate pork for 15 minutes, then thread pork on bamboo skewers.

2 Cook satay over hot coals for 3–4 minutes a side, brushing with oil, until browned. Don't overcook; the meat cooks quickly – and use the marinade to keep the satay moist. Let the satay flare just a little towards the end of cooking to take on a hint of smoke. Alternatively, cook on a preheated barbecue grill rack over medium heat; lower the heat if they flare up too much, or on an oiled barbecue hot plate or in a non-stick frying pan over medium heat. Transfer to a plate when done.

3 To make the dipping sauce, mix all ingredients together in a small bowl. Serve satay with dipping sauce on the side for spooning over.

chicken satay

SERVES 4 (MAKES 12)
TIME TO PREP 20 MINUTES, PLUS 12 HOURS MARINATING
TIME TO COOK 12 MINUTES

KEEP THE PIECES OF CHICKEN SMALL TO ENSURE THEY COOK THROUGH BY THE TIME THEY ARE BROWNED ON THE OUTSIDE. ENHANCE THE LEMONY FLAVOUR BY BRUSHING THE SATAY WITH A SMASHED LEMON GRASS STALK AS THEY COOK. SERVE WITH SPICY SATAY SAUCE (SEE PAGE 144).

1 Put garlic, lemon grass, shallots, oil and coriander seeds in a blender and process to a paste; add 1–2 tablespoons of water if the machine stalls. Cut chicken into small cubes, discarding fat, and put it in a large bowl. Add paste and mix in chilli powder, brown sugar, salt and turmeric. Cover and refrigerate to marinate for 12 hours.

2 Put several chicken pieces on each skewer; I wear disposable gloves to do this because turmeric stains the nails. Cook satay over hot coals for 3–4 minutes a side, brushing the satay often with the lemon grass stalk dipped in oil, until browned and cooked through. Let the satay flare just a little towards the end of cooking to take on a hint of smoke. Alternatively, cook over a preheated barbecue grill rack over medium heat or on an oiled barbecue hot plate or in a ridged grill pan. Transfer to a plate when done and serve immediately.

1 clove garlic, peeled and roughly crushed

large piece lemon grass, trimmed and chopped

½ cup coarsely chopped shallots

2 Tbsp oil, plus extra for basting chicken

1 Tbsp coarsely ground coriander seeds

4 free-range skinned and boned chicken thighs, rinsed and patted dry

½ tsp chilli powder

3 Tbsp brown sugar

½ tsp salt

1 tsp ground turmeric

1 stalk lemon grass, smashed with a mallet for brushing satay

12 bamboo skewers soaked in cold water for 30 minutes

prawns and scallops on skewers

SERVES 2–4 (MAKES 12)
TIME TO PREP 12 MINUTES
TIME TO COOK 5 MINUTES

THIS IS JUST THE TICKET FOR SEAFOOD LOVERS. SERVE IT WITH A BOTTLE OF CHILLED
SAUVIGNON BLANC OR PINOT GRIS FOR A GREAT MATCH.

12 large (raw) green prawns
12 large scallops (about 200g)
6 rashers streaky bacon, thinly
**   sliced**
2 Tbsp olive oil
zest of 1 lemon
1–2 small dried bird's eye chillies,
**   crushed, or ¼ tsp chilli powder**
salt and freshly ground black
**   pepper**
lemon wedges for garnishing

12 small bamboo skewers, soaked in
**   cold water for 30 minutes**

1 If prawns are frozen, thaw them quickly in a sealed plastic bag immersed in a sink of warm water. Twist off their heads, then peel off shells, leaving the small piece of shell on the tail intact. Using a small sharp knife, slice down the back of each prawn and gently extract the red or black vein. Remove any visible black thread on the scallops. Rinse prawns and scallops and pat dry with paper towels.

2 Stretch bacon rashers with the back of a knife and cut each rasher in half. Wrap a piece of bacon around each scallop. Thread the prawns and scallops on bamboo skewers.

3 Put oil, lemon zest, crushed chillies or chilli powder, a few pinches of salt and a little black pepper in a shallow dish and mix together. Add the skewers and turn them to coat evenly with the seasoned oil. Cook skewers on a preheated barbecue hot plate over high heat until bacon is golden, basting with any juices remaining in the dish. Serve garnished with lemon wedges.

rosemary skewers of monkfish and scallops

SERVES 6 (MAKES 12)
TIME TO PREP 30 MINUTES
TIME TO COOK 30 MINUTES

MONKFISH IS DELIGHTFUL WITH SCALLOPS BECAUSE THEY HAVE THE SAME TENDER TEXTURE. IF NOT AVAILABLE, USE LARGE GURNARD FILLETS, OR ANY OTHER WHITE FISH FILLETS. IF LONG-STEMMED ROSEMARY IS NOT AVAILABLE, USE THICK BAMBOO SKEWERS, SOAKED IN WATER FOR 30 MINUTES.

enough long-stemmed rosemary
    for 12 skewers
24 scallops (about 400g)
600g skinned and boned monkfish
    fillets
700g new potatoes
salt
200g slim green beans, trimmed

LEMON VINAIGRETTE
6 Tbsp extra virgin olive oil
2½ Tbsp lemon juice
¾ tsp salt
½ Tbsp finely chopped rosemary
2 cloves garlic, peeled and crushed
1 Tbsp creamy Dijonnaise mustard

1 Cut rosemary stems into 22 centimetre lengths. Remove most of the leaves from the stems; put these in a sealable plastic bag and keep in the refrigerator for other purposes.

2 Remove any visible black threads on the scallops. Rinse scallops and fish and pat dry with paper towels. Cut fish into chunks the same size as the scallops. Thread fish and scallops onto rosemary stems; it may be easier to pierce the scallops and fish first with a metal skewer. Put prepared skewers in a shallow container, cover and refrigerate until 15 minutes before cooking.

3 If the potatoes are freshly dug, scrub to remove loose dirt. If the skins are tough, peel them. Put potatoes in a steaming basket, sprinkle with salt and steam until tender. Alternatively, boil them gently in salted water until tender. Drain and leave until cool enough to handle. Slice hot potatoes and arrange them on individual plates or on a platter; if potatoes are small enough, leave them whole.

4 To make the vinaigrette, whisk ingredients together in a small bowl. Spoon half the vinaigrette over the hot potatoes.

5 Plunge beans into a saucepan of gently boiling, salted water and cook for 3–5 minutes until tender. Drain beans, refresh with a cup or two of cold water, drain well, then tip them onto paper towels. Pat beans dry then add to the potatoes and toss gently. Toss potatoes and beans from time to time as they cool in the vinaigrette.

6 Have fish skewers at room temperature. Spoon half the remaining vinaigrette over and cook skewers on a preheated barbecue grill rack over medium heat, turning carefully. Alternatively, cook them on an oiled barbecue hot plate over medium heat or in a ridged grill pan. (I prefer them on the grill, but you'll need to position them so that the herbaceous part of the skewers is away from any direct flames, or it will flare.) Transfer skewers to the plates or platter of potatoes and beans as they are done, and drizzle with remaining vinaigrette. Serve immediately.

spicy chicken skewers

SERVES 8–12 AS A NIBBLE (MAKES ABOUT 20–30)
TIME TO PREP 15 MINUTES, PLUS 1 HOUR MARINATING
TIME TO COOK 15 MINUTES

MARINATING THESE KEBABS WILL MAKE THEM JUICY AND TENDER.
YOGHURT AND MINT MAKES A GOOD LOW-FAT SAUCE TO GO
WITH THEM.

1 tsp ground cumin
1 clove garlic, peeled and crushed
2 Tbsp lime juice
1 tsp chilli powder
1 tsp honey
1 tsp salt
1 Tbsp oil, plus extra for hot plate
1 Tbsp freshly grated ginger
750g free-range skinned and boned chicken breasts,
   rinsed and patted dry
1 cup plain yoghurt
2 Tbsp chopped mint

20–30 small bamboo skewers, soaked in cold water for
   30 minutes

1 Mix ground cumin, garlic, lime juice, chilli powder,
honey, salt and 1 tablespoon of oil in a large bowl.
Squeeze the grated ginger above the bowl and let the juice
fall into the bowl.

2 Cut chicken into smallish cubes. Put 2–3 pieces of
chicken on each small skewer. Add to bowl of spices and
stir until evenly coated. Transfer them to a shallow container
as they are done. Cover and refrigerate for at least 1 hour,
but up to 24 hours.

3 Cook on a preheated oiled barbecue hot plate over
gentle heat for about 15 minutes until cooked through;
keep the heat gentle, or the skewers will blacken. Brush with
a little oil from time to time during cooking. Alternatively,
cook in an oiled ridged grill pan.

4 Mix yoghurt and mint together and serve with hot
chicken skewers.

prawn skewers

SERVES 4 (MAKES 8)
TIME TO PREP 20 MINUTES
TIME TO COOK 7 MINUTES

THESE ARE QUICKLY BARBECUED ON THE HOT PLATE UNTIL CRISPY.
SERVE WITH CHAMPAGNE OR AN OAKED CHARDONNAY – SUPERB
IS THE ONLY WORD!

24 green (raw) prawns, fresh or frozen
50g butter, melted in a dish
6 Tbsp freshly grated parmesan cheese
2 chorizo sausages, sliced 2–3cm thick
2 juicy lemons, cut into wedges
24 fresh bay leaves
24 large black olives
olive oil for hot plate

8 bamboo skewers, soaked in cold water
   for 30 minutes

1 If prawns are frozen, thaw them quickly in a sealed
plastic bag immersed in a sink of warm water. Twist off
their heads, then peel off shells, leaving the small piece of
shell on the tail intact. Using a small sharp knife, slice down
the back of each prawn and gently extract the red or black
vein. Rinse prawns and pat dry with paper towels.

2 Pass prawns through melted butter then coat them with
parmesan cheese.

3 Thread prawns, chorizo slices, lemon wedges, bay leaves
and olives onto bamboo skewers. The skewers can be
prepared a few hours ahead, but don't stack them. Put them
in a shallow tray lined with baking paper, cover with plastic
food wrap and refrigerate. Bring to room temperature
12–15 minutes before cooking.

4 Cook skewers on a preheated lightly oiled barbecue
hot plate over medium heat until golden. Alternatively,
cook in a smidgin of hot oil in a non-stick frying pan over
medium–high heat. Serve hot and crispy.

greek chicken kebabs

SERVES 4–6 (MAKES ABOUT 12)
TIME TO PREP 20 MINUTES, PLUS 1 HOUR MARINATING
TIME TO COOK 15 MINUTES

THESE KEBABS ARE GUARANTEED TO BE TENDER AND FULL OF FLAVOUR. FOR A CHANGE ADD A LITTLE ROSEMARY OR OREGANO. THEY'RE ESPECIALLY GOOD SERVED WITH PITA POCKETS AND A GREEK SALAD MADE WITH COS LETTUCE LEAVES, TOMATOES, CUCUMBER, RED ONION, FETA AND A GARLICKY, LEMONY DRESSING.

1 large onion, peeled and grated
2 cloves garlic, peeled and crushed
90ml olive oil
juice of 1 lemon
1 tsp smoked Spanish paprika (sweet)
salt and freshly ground black pepper
4 large free-range skinned and boned chicken breasts, rinsed and patted dry

12 bamboo skewers, soaked in cold water for 30 minutes

1 Put onion, garlic, oil, lemon juice, paprika, ½ teaspoon of salt and a good grinding of pepper in a bowl and mix.

2 Cut chicken into small pieces and add to bowl. Toss chicken to coat and cover with plastic food wrap and marinate in the refrigerator for 1–24 hours. Bring to room temperature 10–15 minutes before cooking.

3 Thread chicken on skewers and cook on a preheated barbecue hot plate over medium heat for 12–15 minutes until cooked all the way through. Moisten with marinade as the skewers cook, and keep them sizzling gently. Lower the heat if it is too fierce; slow and sure is the best strategy when cooking chicken. Serve immediately.

prawns with crushed lemon grass and kaffir lime leaves

SERVES 4 (MAKES 8)
TIME TO PREP 12 MINUTES, PLUS 1 HOUR MARINATING
TIME TO COOK 7 MINUTES

SOMEHOW PRAWNS COOKED IN THEIR SHELLS ALWAYS TASTE BETTER EATEN OUTDOORS – MAYBE BECAUSE YOU DON'T HAVE TO STAND ON CEREMONY TO EAT THEM!

16 large green (raw) prawns (about 750g)
10 kaffir lime leaves, centre ribs removed, finely shredded
5 stems lemon grass, smashed with a mallet
1 fresh hot red chilli, halved, deseeded and finely chopped
3 Tbsp olive oil, plus extra for hot plate

8 small bamboo skewers, soaked in cold water for 30 minutes

1 If prawns are frozen, thaw them quickly in a sealed plastic bag immersed in a sink of warm water. Rinse prawns and pat dry with paper towels.

2 Put lime leaves, lemon grass and chilli in a large shallow dish with the oil. Add prawns and coat with marinade. Thread prawns onto skewers. Cover and refrigerate for at least 1 hour, but up to 4 hours. Bring prawns to room temperature 15 minutes before cooking.

3 Cook prawns on a preheated oiled barbecue hot plate over medium–high heat. Tip them, with all the bits and bobs, onto the hot plate and cook until they turn deep coral-pink in colour and the shells lightly golden, then turn them over and cook the other side. Alternatively, cook prawns in a smidgin of hot oil in a non-stick frying pan over medium–high heat. Transfer to a plate. Serve immediately with individual fingerbowls of warm water scented with lemon wedges, and plenty of paper towels for cleaning up!

fish kebabs on warm tomatoes

SERVES 3–4 (MAKES 12)
TIME TO PREP 15 MINUTES
TIME TO COOK 7 MINUTES

THE BRINY TASTE OF GREEN OLIVES GOES WELL WITH AVOCADO OIL AND IS OFFSET
WITH THE SWEET TASTE OF TOMATOES AND PEPPERY ANISE FLAVOUR OF BASIL. THE KEBABS
CAN BE SKEWERED SEVERAL HOURS AHEAD. SERVE THEM WITH CRUSTY BREAD AND A
ROCKET SALAD.

1 Cut the peel off lemons in long thick strips. Rinse fish and pat dry with paper towels. Cut fish into cubes about the same size as the olives. Thread fish on skewers with olives, bay leaves and strips of lemon peel. Lay the kebabs in a dish and drizzle with a little olive oil.

2 Cook fish kebabs on a preheated oiled barbecue hot plate over medium heat until fish is lightly browned and just cooked through; do not overcook. Alternatively, cook kebabs in a ridged grill pan over medium heat.

3 Meanwhile, put avocado or olive oil in a large frying pan. Halve the tomatoes and lay them cut side down in the pan. Season with sea salt and pepper. Set the pan over low heat and let them warm through for about 5 minutes, until they show signs of softening. (The pan of tomatoes could also be warmed through over the barbecue hot plate if you wish to do all the cooking outside.) Slide tomatoes onto a large serving platter, or individual plates, scatter over basil and top with the hot kebabs. Serve immediately.

2 lemons
500g skinned and boned gurnard fillets (or any other firm-textured fish that will hold together well)
1 cup pimiento-stuffed green olives, drained
12 fresh bay leaves
olive oil, plus extra for hot plate
2 Tbsp extra virgin avocado or olive oil
12 smallish vine tomatoes
sea salt and freshly ground black pepper
½ cup basil leaves

12 bamboo skewers, soaked in cold water for 30 minutes

*Go to www.juliebiuso.com
for a video clip of Julie
demonstrating this recipe.*

tiger prawns with mixed leaf salad and sizzled lychees

SERVES 6 (MAKES 12)
TIME TO PREP 25 MINUTES
TIME TO COOK 7 MINUTES

JUICY LYCHEES ARE GORGEOUS WITH PRAWNS. IF YOU DON'T BELIEVE ME, TRY MAKING THESE LITTLE BEAUTIES AND SEE FOR YOURSELF!

1kg green (raw) tiger prawns or 20–24 large green (raw) prawns
50g butter
2 small dried bird's eye chillies, crushed
olive oil for hot plate

SALAD
3 cups micro or baby salad greens
½ cup very fresh bean sprouts, trimmed
1 cup coriander leaves
½ cup small mint leaves
2 Tbsp lime juice
½ tsp fish sauce
pinch caster sugar
1 x 565g can lychees, drained

12 bamboo skewers, soaked for 30 minutes in cold water

1 If prawns are frozen, thaw them quickly in a sealed plastic bag immersed in a sink of warm water. Twist off their heads, then peel off shells, leaving the small piece of shell on the tail intact. Using a small sharp knife, slice down the back of each prawn and gently extract the red or black vein. Rinse prawns and pat dry with paper towels.

2 Melt butter in a shallow dish and mix in crushed chillies. Toss prawns in chilli butter then thread 3 prawns on each skewer. The prawns can be prepared several hours ahead, covered and refrigerated.

3 Prepare the salad greens and herbs and put them in plastic bags or in bowls covered with plastic food wrap in the refrigerator until ready to serve.

4 Put lime juice, fish sauce and sugar in a large bowl and stir until sugar dissolves.

5 Cook prawns on a preheated oiled barbecue hot plate over medium heat until golden. Turn prawns over once they start turning pink. At the same time, sizzle lychees in the buttery juices that come out of the prawns, until they are just heated through and lightly browned. Transfer to a plate once they are done. Alternatively, cook prawns in a non-stick frying pan over medium heat and sizzle the lychees at the same time in a separate lightly oiled pan.

6 To serve, put the salad greens and herbs in a bowl and pour on the dressing. Toss together and serve with the prawns and lychees.

chicken and pineapple skewers with pomegranate molasses

SERVES 4 (MAKES ABOUT 16)
TIME TO PREP 25 MINUTES
TIME TO COOK 15 MINUTES

IF LIME LEAVES ARE NOT AVAILABLE USE LEAVES FROM AN UNSPRAYED LEMON TREE OR THICK STRIPS OF LEMON PEEL INSTEAD.

3 free-range skinned and boned chicken breasts, rinsed and patted dry
1 large red pepper (capsicum)
½ fresh pineapple
1 x 227g can water chestnuts, drained
8 kaffir lime leaves, halved
olive oil for hot plate
sea salt
pomegranate molasses for drizzling
steamed rice for serving

16–20 bamboo skewers, soaked in cold water for 30 minutes

1 Cut chicken breasts into strips then into smallish cubes. Halve red pepper and remove core, seeds and white membrane. Cut red pepper into squares the same size as the cubes of the chicken. Cut off pineapple skin, remove core and cut flesh into cubes the same size as the chicken.

2 Thread chicken on skewers with red pepper, pineapple, water chestnuts and lime leaves. The chicken skewers can be assembled several hours ahead, covered and refrigerated until required, but bring to room temperature 12–15 minutes before cooking.

3 Cook chicken skewers on a preheated oiled barbecue hot plate over a low–medium heat; if you cook them too quickly the other ingredients will char before the chicken is cooked through; slow and sure is the best way. Turn them from time to time, and cook until lightly golden and the chicken is just cooked through. The skewers can also be cooked indoors in a ridged grill pan. Transfer skewers to a platter as they are done, and sprinkle with a little sea salt. When all are ready, drizzle with pomegranate molasses and serve immediately with a bowl of steamed rice.

beef, yellow peppers and shallots on sticks

SERVES 4–6 (MAKES 20)
TIME TO PREP 30 MINUTES, PLUS 1 HOUR MARINATING
TIME TO COOK 10 MINUTES

CUTTING STEAK INTO CUBES AND SPEARING IT ON SKEWERS WITH OTHER INGREDIENTS MAKES IT GO FURTHER. YOU COULD ALSO REPLACE THE BEEF WITH CHICKEN IF YOU PREFER, BUT KEEP THE CUBES OF CHICKEN THE SAME SIZE AS THE VEGETABLES AND ENSURE THE PIECES ARE COOKED ALL THE WAY THROUGH.

300g shallots
2 large yellow peppers (capsicums)
750g scotch fillet
12 fresh bay leaves, optional
3 Tbsp olive oil, plus extra for hot plate
1 Tbsp dried oregano
1 Tbsp creamy Dijonnaise mustard
½ tsp salt
½ tsp freshly ground black pepper

20 large bamboo skewers, soaked in cold water for 30 minutes

1 Peel shallots and break apart into separate bulbs. Cut each bulb in half, or into quarters (so they are roughly the size of a large stuffed olive). Halve the peppers, remove cores and seeds and cut into small chunks roughly the same size as shallots. Trim beef of any fat and any silvery skin and cut meat into cubes a little larger than the pepper cubes and shallots. Thread meat, bay leaves and vegetables onto skewers.

2 Mix oil, oregano, mustard, salt and plenty of black pepper in a shallow dish and add the skewers. Turn skewers in the marinade and let them marinate for 1–2 hours, turning occasionally.

3 Cook skewers over medium heat on a lightly oiled barbecue hot plate, turning often, until everything is browned and smelling appetising. Serve immediately.

served in a bowl

Wok it, stir-fry it or stick it on the grill, add grains, pulses, salad or

vegetables then serve in a bowl: fresh punchy flavours to

arrest your palate.

chilli beef with lime and palm sugar dressing

SERVES 6
TIME TO PREP 35 MINUTES
TIME TO COOK 25 MINUTES

HERE'S THE QUINTESSENTIAL WESTERNISED THAI BEEF SALAD. JUST THE THING FOR HOT
WEATHER BUT THE BEEF IS COOKED IN THE OVEN RATHER THAN ON THE BARBECUE.

800g piece fillet steak, taken from the fat end of the fillet, at room temperature
1½ Tbsp oil
salt and freshly ground black pepper

DRESSING
3 Tbsp light vegetable oil
2 Tbsp fresh lime juice
2 tsp fish sauce
1 tsp salt
1 tsp grated or crushed palm sugar or raw sugar
1 clove garlic, peeled and very finely chopped
juice squeezed from 2 Tbsp coarsely grated ginger
1 fresh hot red chilli, halved, deseeded and very finely chopped
2 fresh limes

VEGETABLES
70g snow peas or sugar snaps (less than 1 cup)
½ an iceberg lettuce, torn into bite-sized pieces
2 cups very fresh bean sprouts, trimmed, optional
1 telegraph cucumber, peeled and thinly sliced
½ cup mint leaves
½ cup coriander leaves
¼ cup Thai basil leaves, optional

1 Trim away fat and silverskin from beef, then tie with string so that it holds its shape while cooking. Heat oil in a heavy-based casserole over medium–high heat, and when the oil is nice and hot add beef and brown well on both sides. Sprinkle generously with salt and grind over plenty of black pepper. Transfer casserole to an oven preheated to 200°C (fanbake) and roast for 15 minutes, turning once. Remove meat from oven, cool, then cover and refrigerate for 1–2 hours or more. Slice beef thinly, stack the slices in a container, cover with plastic food wrap and refrigerate; the beef will regain its red colour when it is taken from the refrigerator and slices are separated.

2 To make the dressing, mix the vegetable oil in a bowl with the lime juice, fish sauce, salt, sugar, garlic, ginger juice and chilli. Peel the limes with a serrated knife, then slice in between each piece of membrane and release the lime fillets. Cut them into small pieces and add to the dressing along with any juice; squeeze the juice from the membrane into the bowl as well.

3 To prepare the vegetables, first blanch the snow peas by dropping them into a saucepan of gently boiling water for 30 seconds. Drain and rinse with cold water until cool, then pat dry. If cooking sugar snaps, leave them in the water for 2 minutes. Put the lettuce, snow peas or sugar snaps, bean sprouts, if using, and cucumber in a large bowl and scatter over most of the herbs. Spoon some dressing over the salad. Toss well and serve into 6 bowls. Arrange the beef on top of the salads, scatter with the rest of the herbs and spoon the rest of the dressing over. Toss each salad lightly and serve immediately.

lamb and aubergine salad with chickpeas and roasted tomatoes

SERVES 6
TIME TO PREP 20 MINUTES
TIME TO COOK 25 MINUTES

LAMB AND AUBERGINE IS A LEGENDARY COMBINATION – THINK MOUSSAKA – BUT IT'S EVEN BETTER WITH THE TANG OF TOMATOES AND PUNCH OF GARLIC AND LEMON. LAMB BACKSTRAPS AREN'T CHEAP (THEY'RE A PRIME CUT), BUT IN A SALAD LIKE THIS, A LITTLE RED MEAT GOES A LONG WAY.

ROASTED TOMATOES

10 smallish vine tomatoes, halved
sugar
sea salt
2 Tbsp coarsely ground coriander seeds
1 tsp freshly ground lemon or black pepper
lemon-infused extra virgin olive oil or use regular extra virgin olive oil

SALAD

1 aubergine (eggplant)
olive oil
sea salt and freshly ground black pepper
several sprigs of rosemary
4 lamb backstraps (about 700g)
1 x 325g jar or 400g can chickpeas, drained, rinsed and drained
1 large clove garlic, peeled and crushed
1 Tbsp lemon juice
1 Tbsp extra virgin olive oil
130g rocket, trimmed
100g feta, drained, mopped dry and sliced, optional
20 kalamata olives
lemon wedges for garnishing

Go to www.juliebiuso.com for a video clip of Julie demonstrating this recipe.

1 To roast the tomatoes, put them cut side up in a shallow ovenproof dish lined with baking paper. (A Swiss roll tin is ideal.) Sprinkle with a little sugar, then season with a little sea salt, freshly ground coriander seeds and lemon pepper. Drizzle with a little lemon oil or olive oil. Bake in an oven preheated to 225°C (fanbake) for 15 minutes, or until tomatoes are just starting to char around the edges and starting to collapse.

2 To make the salad, cut aubergine lengthways into long thin slices. Put a little oil on a large plate and dunk aubergine slices one at a time in the oil, letting excess oil drip off. Transfer them to a barbecue grill rack heated to medium. Cook quickly until tender, golden and lightly charred around the edges; you'll need to move the slices around often as they cook to prevent scorching. Transfer aubergine slices to a clean plate as they are done and season with sea salt. Repeat with remaining aubergine slices. Alternatively, cook aubergine slices in a ridged frying pan over medium–high heat.

3 Put rosemary sprigs in a shallow dish with 1 tablespoon of olive oil. Trim lamb, removing silvery skin. Add to dish and turn to coat it in the oil and rosemary. Grind over a little black pepper. Cook lamb on a preheated barbecue hot plate over medium heat for 2–3 minutes each side. It should be nicely brown but remain medium–rare inside; it will continue to cook as it stands before slicing. Transfer to a board and sprinkle generously with salt. Let lamb rest at least 5 minutes before slicing. Alternatively, cook lamb in a ridged grill pan over medium–high heat.

4 Toss chickpeas in a small bowl with garlic and lemon juice and extra virgin olive oil, adding a pinch or two of salt and a good grinding of black pepper.

5 Divide rocket between 6 serving bowls and distribute aubergine slices over the top. Slice lamb, then let it rest for a few minutes before adding to the bowls with chickpeas and all the garlicky juices, tomatoes, feta if using, and olives. Toss each salad very gently, then garnish with lemon wedges and serve.

couscous with aubergine

SERVES 6
TIME TO PREP 20 MINUTES
TIME TO COOK 15 MINUTES

THIS IS A GREAT VEGETARIAN DISH, BUT IT CAN BE SERVED TO ACCOMPANY MEAT
DISHES, TOO.

1 Put the couscous in a bowl and pour over the boiling water. Stir once, then cover and leave for 10 minutes. Fluff up with a fork, cover again and leave until cool.

2 Cut aubergine lengthways into long thin slices. Put a little oil on a large plate and dunk aubergine slices one at a time in the oil, letting excess oil drip off. Transfer them to a barbecue grill rack heated to medium. Cook quickly until tender and golden and lightly charred around the edges; you'll need to move the slices around often as they cook to prevent scorching. Transfer aubergine slices to a clean plate as they are done and season them with sea salt. Repeat with remaining aubergine slices. Alternatively, cook aubergine slices in a ridged grill pan heated to medium–high.

3 Put pine nuts in a small dry frying pan over medium heat and let them toast until a pale nut brown; shake the pan from time to time to encourage them to brown evenly. Tip them onto a side plate to cool.

4 Blanch beans in a saucepan of gently boiling salted water for a few minutes until they just lose their raw crunch. Drain and refresh with cold water, then pat dry with paper towels.

5 To make the dressing, mix all ingredients together and pour onto couscous. Mix thoroughly. Add currants, pine nuts, beans, chickpeas and tomatoes and toss together. Grind over a little black pepper. Heap couscous in a mound on a serving plate and surround with the aubergine slices. Alternatively, dish into individual bowls for serving.

200g (1 cup) couscous
250ml boiling water
1 medium-sized aubergine (eggplant)
olive oil
sea salt and freshly ground black pepper
3 Tbsp pine nuts
250g green beans, trimmed and cut into short lengths
2 Tbsp currants
1 x 325g jar or 400g can chickpeas, drained, rinsed and drained
1 cup cherry tomatoes, halved

DRESSING
3 Tbsp extra virgin olive oil
1 Tbsp lemon juice
1 fresh hot red chilli, halved, deseeded and finely chopped
1 large clove garlic, peeled and crushed
2 Tbsp chopped flat-leaf parsley or coriander
½ tsp salt

green chicken curry with cashew nuts

SERVES 6
TIME TO PREP 25 MINUTES
TIME TO COOK 1 HOUR, 15–30 MINUTES

THERE'S BAGS OF FLAVOUR HERE, BUT CHECK THE TIMINGS – IT'S PROBABLY MORE SUITED
TO A NIGHT WHEN YOU'VE GOT A BIT OF TIME ON YOUR HANDS AND ARE COOKING
INDOORS, RATHER THAN ONE OF THOSE NIGHTS WHEN THE SPEED OF A WOK MEAL COULD
SERVE YOU BETTER.

CASHEW-NUT CURRY PASTE

2 large onions, peeled and finely sliced

3 Tbsp canola or peanut oil

½ cup roasted, salted cashew nuts

6 large cloves garlic, peeled and halved

1 cup loosely packed coriander leaves

1 cup loosely packed mint leaves

4 fresh hot green chillies, coarsely chopped

CURRY

50g tamarind pulp

½ cup hot water

3 Tbsp canola or peanut oil

1 Tbsp peeled, grated ginger

2 fresh hot green chillies, deseeded and finely chopped

1kg free-range skinned and boned chicken thighs, rinsed, patted dry and halved

1 tsp salt

plain yoghurt for serving

1 sliced fresh red chilli for serving

chopped coriander leaves and mint for serving

1 To make the cashew-nut paste, fry onions gently in 2 tablespoons of oil in a medium-sized frying pan for 40–45 minutes until they caramelise; stir often, especially towards the end of cooking time.

2 While the onions are cooking, soak the cashew nuts in warm water to soften for 10 minutes. Drain and pat dry.

3 Fry garlic cloves in a small pan in 1 tablespoon of oil for a few minutes until lightly coloured. Transfer to a food processor with the cashew nuts, onions, coriander, mint and chillies and process to a paste.

4 To make the curry, put tamarind pulp in a small bowl and pour in hot water. Leave to soften for 5 minutes, then use your fingers to separate the pulp from the seeds. Push the mixture through a sieve and discard seeds and tough fibre.

5 Heat oil over a gentle heat in a casserole, and add ginger and green chillies. Fry for 1–2 minutes then add the cashew-nut paste. Fry for 5 minutes, stirring, then add chicken. Lightly brown chicken then add tamarind liquid and mix in.

6 Cover casserole with a lid and simmer very gently for about 20 minutes, or until the chicken is cooked. If the thighs are large they may take more than 30 minutes to cook through; add a little water if the sauce gets dry. Season chicken with salt then tip into a serving dish, scraping in all the sauce, or simply serve in the casserole. Pour over a little yoghurt and garnish with sliced red chilli and chopped coriander and mint. Serve piping hot.

grilled squid salad

SERVES 4
TIME TO PREP 25 MINUTES
TIME TO COOK 5 MINUTES

IF PREPARING THE SQUID IS ALL TOO MUCH, ASK YOUR
FISHMONGER TO DO IT FOR YOU OR BUY READY-PREPARED FROZEN
SQUID TUBES.

4 medium-sized squid
5 Tbsp extra virgin olive oil
½ tsp freshly ground black pepper
2 cloves garlic, peeled and crushed
3 tiny dried chillies, crushed
1 lemon
130g baby rocket leaves
1 Tbsp marjoram leaves
2 medium-sized vine tomatoes, diced, cubed and
**   drained**
1 Tbsp lemon juice
¼ tsp salt

1 Prepare the squid one at a time. Firstly, remove the quill (transparent spine) by running a finger along the inside of the pocket to loosen it. Hold the tip of the quill in one hand and the head in the other and gently pull on the quill so as not to break the ink sac; most of the guts, including the ink sac, should come out in one neat pile. Remove the wings, transparent purple-ish skin and beak. (The quill and beak look like pieces of plastic.) Cut the tentacles off. Give the tube a final clean by turning it inside-out and washing off any remaining goo.

2 Cut each squid pocket along one side to open it up and cut each in half again lengthways. Score the inside of each piece of squid into a diamond pattern with the point of a small sharp knife. Cut the squid into fat fingers. Cut tentacles into smaller pieces, if large. Put squid in a bowl and pour over 2 tablespoons of the oil. Grind on black pepper and add garlic and crushed chillies. Toss to coat them with the marinade.

3 Peel all the skin and white pith from the lemon using a small serrated knife. Cut in between each piece of membrane and let the lemon segments fall onto a board.

Cut each segment into 3 pieces. Put rocket in a bowl with lemon segments, marjoram leaves and diced tomato.

4 Barbecue squid pieces for 2–3 minutes each side on a preheated barbecue hot plate until the pieces curl and are lightly coloured; do not overcook. Alternatively, cook squid in a non-stick pan over high heat.

5 Lightly toss the rocket leaves, marjoram and tomatoes with remaining oil and lemon juice and season with salt. Serve into 4 bowls and pile the barbecued squid on top. Serve immediately.

summer fish

SERVES 6
TIME TO PREP 25 MINUTES
TIME TO COOK 40 MINUTES

THIS IS AN IMPRESSIVE DISH WITH PLENTY OF FLAVOUR. YOU CAN
START COOKING IT INSIDE AND FINISH IT OFF ON THE BARBECUE.

700g desiree potatoes or small freshly dug
**   waxy potatoes**
salt
3 sweet corn cobs, husks and silks removed
1 Tbsp olive oil, plus extra for hot plate
300g free-range middle bacon, trimmed and cubed
1 large onion, peeled and finely chopped
salt and freshly ground black pepper
2 ripe but firm avocados
juice of ½ a lemon
20 cherry tomatoes
700g skinned and boned white fish fillets (gurnard,
**   snapper, red mullet or bream)**
½ cup basil leaves, shredded, plus a handful of tiny
**   basil leaves for garnishing**
lemon-infused extra virgin olive oil for drizzling

1 Peel desiree potatoes or scrub freshly dug waxy potatoes. Cut into large chunks and put in a saucepan. Cover with cold water, salt lightly and bring to the boil. Lower the heat and cook gently for about 12 minutes, until

just tender when pierced with a skewer. Drain potatoes and return them to the wiped-out dry pan and set the pan back on the heat briefly to dry off clinging moisture. Cook sweet corn in gently boiling unsalted water for 5 minutes, then drain.

2 Heat oil in a large frying pan and add bacon and potatoes. Cook over medium–high heat for about 10 minutes, stirring often, until bacon is crisp. Add onion and cook for 5 minutes more or until golden. Season with salt and pepper.

3 Cook corn cobs on a preheated oiled barbecue hot plate over medium heat until lightly golden. Alternatively, cook corn in a lightly oiled non-stick frying pan. As soon as cool enough to handle, slice kernels off cobs. Halve avocados, remove stones, then peel. Slice thickly and sprinkle with lemon juice and season with a little salt and pepper. Halve tomatoes and season with a little salt and pepper.

4 Rinse fish fillets and pat dry with paper towels. Cut each fillet into 2–3 pieces. Cook fish fillets on a preheated oiled barbecue hot plate over medium heat until golden. Flip fish over and cook the other side briefly, just to seal. Alternatively, cook fish in a little oil in a frying pan until browned and barely cooked through. Transfer fish fillets to a plate and let them rest for a few minutes.

5 Spoon bacon, potatoes and onion mixture into 6 bowls and layer with avocado slices, cherry tomatoes, sweet corn kernels and shredded basil. Top with warm fish fillets, season with a little salt and pepper, drizzle lightly with lemon infused olive oil and scatter tiny basil leaves on top. Serve immediately.

hot and sour pork

SERVES 4–6
TIME TO PREP 35 MINUTES
TIME TO COOK 5–10 MINUTES

THIS IS AN EASY DISH BECAUSE EVERYTHING CAN BE PREPARED AHEAD. THE KEY IS TO ENSURE THE BARBECUE IS VERY HOT WHEN YOU ARE READY TO COOK AND TO RESIST TEMPTATION TO TURN THE PORK BEFORE IT IS NICELY BROWNED.

1 small red onion, peeled
700g piece free-range pork fillet
2 Tbsp canola or peanut oil
salt
1 telegraph cucumber
8 large leaves iceberg lettuce, torn into
   bite-sized pieces
20 cherry tomatoes, halved
150g (about 2 cups) very fresh bean sprouts, trimmed
1 cup fresh coriander leaves
1 cup small mint leaves

DRESSING
finely grated zest 1 lime
90ml lime juice
1½ Tbsp grated palm sugar or brown sugar
1½ Tbsp fish sauce
2 fresh hot red chillies, finely chopped

1 Cut onion into slivers and soak in icy cold water for 15 minutes. Drain and pat dry.

2 Remove any fat from pork fillet, slice reasonably thinly (not into slivers, just nice and thin) then toss in a bowl with oil. Cook pork on a preheated barbecue hot plate over high heat, until browned and barely cooked through (the pork will continue to cook as it stands). Transfer to a plate and season with a little salt.

3 Peel cucumber and cut in half lengthways, then into slices. Arrange iceberg lettuce on a platter with cucumber, cherry tomatoes, bean sprouts, red onion, coriander and mint leaves.

4 To make the dressing, put all the ingredients in a bowl and stir until sugar dissolves. Arrange pork on top of the salad, pour dressing over and toss gently. Dish into bowls and serve immediately.

5 Arrange pork on top of the salad, pour dressing over and toss gently. Dish into bowls and serve immediately.

vietnamese herb salad with fish

SERVES 4
TIME TO PREP 25 MINUTES
TIME TO COOK 7 MINUTES

LOVELY CLEAN FLAVOURS MAKE THIS DISH IDEAL FOR SUMMER DINING AND IT'S EVEN
BETTER IF YOU HAVE CAUGHT THE FISH YOURSELF! IF YOU WANT TO MAKE THE DISH
LIGHTER, STEAM THE FISH INSTEAD OF BARBECUING IT.

½ large telegraph cucumber
1 bunch spring onions
⅓ cup small mint leaves (if large,
   tear into small pieces)
½ cup coriander leaves
500g skinned and boned white
   fish fillets (gurnard, snapper, red
   mullet or bream)
canola or peanut oil for hot plate
salt
¼ cup dry-roasted peanuts,
   chopped, optional

DRESSING
3 Tbsp fish sauce
5 Tbsp lime juice
2 Tbsp sugar
1 fresh hot red chilli, finely chopped
1 large clove garlic, peeled and
   finely chopped
1 Tbsp peeled and finely grated
   ginger

1 Peel cucumber, cut in half lengthways, scoop out seeds with a pointy teaspoon and cut flesh into half moon shapes. Trim spring onions, discarding most of the greenery and cut into long, thin strips. Put spring onions in a bowl with cucumber, mint and coriander. Cover and chill.

2 To make the dressing, whisk everything together in a small bowl. Cover and chill.

3 Rinse fish and pat dry with paper towels. Cook fish on a preheated oiled barbecue hot plate over medium heat until golden. Flip fish over and cook the second side briefly, just to seal. Alternatively, cook fish in a little oil in a large frying pan until lightly browned and barely cooked through or steam it. Transfer to a platter as it is done, cool for 5 minutes, then pour off liquid. When all the fish is ready, season lightly with salt and transfer to bowls for serving.

4 Mix salad and dressing together and arrange on top of the fish in the bowls. Sprinkle peanuts on top, if using, and serve immediately.

speedy beef stir-fry

SERVES 2 (OR 1 VERY HUNGRY TEENAGER)
TIME TO PREP 15 MINUTES
TIME TO COOK 5 MINUTES

THIS WAS ONE OF MY SON LUCA'S FAVOURITE STIR-FRIES TO COOK IN HIS TEENAGE YEARS. IT CAME FROM JANYA, MY CHINESE ASSISTANT AT THE TIME. IT'S FAST AND DRAMATIC – THERE'S LOTS OF ACTION AND HEAPS OF FLAVOUR! FOR A COMPLETE MEAL, JUST ADD RICE.

200g rump steak or scotch fillet, sliced
1 tsp cornflour
1 Tbsp soy sauce
½ tsp sesame oil
2 Tbsp canola or peanut oil
2 cloves garlic, peeled and chopped
1 Tbsp peeled and grated ginger
1 red pepper (capsicum), halved, cored, deseeded and sliced
3 spring onions, trimmed and sliced into short lengths
2 small courgettes (zucchini), trimmed and cut into chunks
¼ tsp salt
1 Tbsp oyster sauce
2 Tbsp water

1 Put sliced steak in a bowl with cornflour, soy sauce and sesame oil. Mix thoroughly.

2 Heat a wok over high heat, then add the oil. When the oil is nice and hot, add steak and fry until browned. Add garlic, ginger and vegetables. Season with a little salt and stir through oyster sauce and, finally, add water.

3 Turn contents of wok into a heated bowl and serve immediately.

seared scallops on warm fregola salad

SERVES 4 GENEROUSLY AS A STARTER, OR ADD EXTRA
SEAFOOD FOR A MAIN COURSE
TIME TO PREP 15 MINUTES
TIME TO COOK 25 MINUTES

FREGOLA IS A SMALL TYPE OF PASTA HAILING FROM SARDINIA. IF IT'S NOT AVAILABLE, USE ORZO (RICE-SHAPED PASTA) INSTEAD.

2 yellow peppers (capsicums), halved, cored, deseeded and diced
3½ Tbsp extra virgin olive oil
1 cup fregola or ¾ cup orzo
1 Tbsp creamy Dijonnaise mustard
salt and freshly ground black pepper
250g scallops, trimmed, rinsed and patted dry
½ cup small basil leaves

1 Put yellow peppers in a frying pan with 2 tablespoons of the oil and cook gently for about 10 minutes or until the peppers have softened. Transfer them to a bowl with all the juices.

2 Cook fregola for about 10 minutes, until al dente, in gently boiling salted water or according to instructions on the packet; if using orzo, cook for about 5 minutes. Drain fregola or orzo and add to the peppers. Mix the mustard, 1 tablespoon of oil, a little black pepper and a good few pinches of salt together in a small bowl, then stir it through the pasta and peppers. Pile the salad into a heated bowl.

3 Put scallops in a bowl and drizzle over ½ a tablespoon of oil. Toss gently until they are coated in oil. Cook scallops briefly on a preheated barbecue hot plate over medium heat for about 45 seconds a side until lightly browned and just cooked through. Alternatively, cook scallops in a ridged grill pan heated until nice and hot; don't crowd the pan and cook in batches, if necessary. Cook them on both sides for 1 minute, as above. Transfer scallops to a dish as they are done. When all are ready, stir the basil through the salad and dish into bowls. Spoon the scallops on top and serve immediately.

green mango and smoked chicken salad with cellophane noodles

SERVES 4 AS A STARTER OR LIGHT SALAD
TIME TO PREP 35 MINUTES
TIME TO COOK 20 MINUTES

IT'S PROBABLY NOT KOSHER TO SNIP NOODLES WITH SCISSORS
– LONG NOODLES REPRESENT LONG LIFE IN CHINA – BUT IT SURE
MAKES EATING CELLOPHANE NOODLES A LOT EASIER!

100g cellophane noodles
2 free-range skinned and boned chicken breasts
1 Tbsp canola or peanut oil, plus extra for hot plate
sea salt
1 unripe mango
1 slim carrot
½ small telegraph cucumber
½ cup lightly packed coriander leaves
2 Tbsp fried shallots
2 fresh hot red chillies, chopped

DRESSING
1½ Tbsp fish sauce
4 Tbsp lime juice
1½ tsp caster sugar
1 Tbsp finely chopped shallot
1 fresh hot red chilli, halved, deseeded and
  finely chopped
pinch of salt

1 Boil a kettle of water and leave to cool for 10 minutes. Put cellophane noodles in a bowl and pour on cooled, boiled water to cover. Leave noodles to soften for about 7 minutes or until just tender but still a little resilient. Drain, rinse under running cold water and drain again. Pass the scissors through the noodles several times to make them shorter in length and more manageable to eat.

2 Put chicken breasts in a shallow dish and pour on oil. Cook chicken breast on a preheated lightly oiled barbecue hot plate over medium heat until a good golden colour and cooked through. The chicken breasts should sizzle along nicely; don't let the barbecue get too hot or they will dry out. Alternatively, cook chicken breasts in a little hot oil over medium heat in a ridged frying pan. Season them with salt and transfer to a plate to cool. Once the chicken breasts are cool enough to handle, slice meat into long strips against the grain.

3 Peel mango, then cut off mango cheeks and any other flesh. Discard the seed and slice flesh finely. Peel carrot and cut into thin shavings with a potato peeler. Peel cucumber, cut in half and scoop out the seeds with a pointy teaspoon. Slice cucumber into half moon shapes and put in a bowl with mango and carrot.

4 To make the dressing, mix all ingredients together in a small bowl and pour dressing over the mango mixture. Add chicken, coriander leaves and noodles and carefully toss together. Taste, and if it is too sweet add more lime juice and add a pinch more salt, if necessary. Garnish with shallots and chopped chilli and serve immediately.

seared vine tomatoes with feta

SERVES 4
TIME TO PREP 7 MINUTES
TIME TO COOK 5 MINUTES

THIS SALAD CAN BE TOPPED WITH GRILLED CHICKEN BREASTS
FOR A MORE SUBSTANTIAL MEAL, AND IT'S EVEN MORE DELICIOUS
DRIZZLED WITH LEMON-INFUSED EXTRA VIRGIN OLIVE OIL.

12 medium-sized vine tomatoes, halved
extra virgin olive oil
sea salt and freshly ground black pepper
caster sugar
4 cups rocket leaves or salad greens, picked over
200g firm feta, mopped dry and sliced
1 juicy lemon

1 Put tomatoes on a large plate and drizzle with a little oil and season with salt, pepper and a pinch or two of sugar. Cook tomatoes cut side down on a preheated barbecue hot plate over medium heat for 3–5 minutes until lightly browned. Turn tomatoes over and cook for 1 minute more.

2 Pile rocket or salad greens into bowls and arrange feta and tomatoes on top. Squeeze over a little lemon juice, drizzle with oil and grind on black pepper to taste. Serve immediately with crunchy bread.

vietnamese pork balls with fresh herb salad

SERVES 4–6 (MAKES 30 PORK BALLS)
TIME TO PREP 30 MINUTES, PLUS AT LEAST 1 HOUR
  CHILLING
TIME TO COOK 7–10 MINUTES

THIS SALAD MAKES A FRESH AND HEALTHY ACCOMPANIMENT TO
CHICKEN AND FISH AS WELL AS PORK. REMEMBER THE BEST MINCE
IS FRESH MINCE – SHOP FOR IT THE DAY YOU PLAN TO COOK IT.

PORK BALLS
500g minced free-range pork
¼ cup panko crumbs
6 kaffir lime leaves, centre ribs removed, finely
  shredded
3 cloves garlic, peeled and crushed
1 Tbsp peeled and grated ginger
1 fresh hot red chilli, finely chopped
2 Tbsp fish sauce
2 spring onions, trimmed and chopped

HERB SALAD
1 cup very fresh bean sprouts, trimmed
½ telegraph cucumber, thinly sliced
1 cup coriander leaves
½ cup mint leaves
2 cups micro cress or torn cos or iceberg lettuce leaves
4 Tbsp white vinegar
1 fresh hot red chilli, finely chopped
2 Tbsp chopped shallots

olive oil for hot plate
steamed rice for serving
toasted coconut flakes for garnishing
sliced fresh red chilli for garnishing

1 To make the pork balls, put all the ingredients in a bowl and squelch together; I wear disposable food gloves to do this. Shape into 30 small balls, putting them on a tray as they are done. Cover and refrigerate for 1 hour, or longer. Bring pork balls to room temperature before cooking.

2 Cook pork balls on a preheated oiled barbecue hot plate over medium heat until golden brown and cooked through. Alternatively, cook in a little oil in a non-stick frying pan. Transfer to a plate as they are done.

3 To make the salad, put the bean sprouts, cucumber, herbs and micro cress or lettuce leaves in a bowl and toss lightly. Mix the vinegar, fresh chilli and shallots together in a small dish and add to salad. Toss lightly.

4 Serve pork balls on steamed rice garnished with coconut and fresh chilli. Serve the herb salad separately.

lamb salad with bean sprouts and cucumber

SERVES 2–3
TIME TO PREP 25 MINUTES
TIME TO COOK 7 MINUTES

THIS LAMB SALAD HAS PLENTY OF BITE AND IS PERFECT FOR
2–3 PEOPLE, NOT A CROWD.

1–2 Tbsp olive oil
2 lamb backstraps (about 350g)
¼ tsp freshly ground black pepper
½ tsp salt
⅓ telegraph cucumber, peeled and thinly sliced
1 cup very fresh bean sprouts, trimmed
6 slim spring onions, trimmed and sliced
2 cloves garlic, peeled and finely chopped
2 kaffir lime leaves, centre ribs removed, finely
   shredded
2 fresh hot red chillies, finely chopped or sliced

DRESSING
3 Tbsp lime juice
1 Tbsp sugar
1 Tbsp fish sauce

1 Put oil in a shallow dish. Trim lamb, removing any silvery skin. Add to dish and turn to coat it in the oil. Grind over a little black pepper. Cook lamb on a preheated barbecue hot plate over medium heat for 2–3 minutes each side. It should be nicely brown but remain medium–rare inside; don't overcook, it will continue to cook as it stands before slicing. Transfer to a board and sprinkle generously with salt. Let lamb rest at least 5 minutes before slicing. Alternatively, cook lamb in a ridged grill pan over medium–high heat. Slice lamb against the grain once it is cool.

2 Layer up cucumber, bean sprouts, spring onions, garlic, kaffir lime leaves, chillies and sliced lamb in individual shallow bowls.

3 To make the dressing, mix all ingredients together in a small ramekin and pour over the salads. Toss gently and serve immediately.

thai prawn and noodle salad

SERVES 6
TIME TO PREP 30 MINUTES
TIME TO COOK 7–10 MINUTES

THIS IS A GOOD, STANDARD PRAWN STIR-FRY, PERFECT FOR
MID-WEEK DINING.

100g rice stick noodles
12–16 green (raw) prawns
2 Tbsp canola or peanut oil
70g slim green beans, trimmed and sliced into strips
1 carrot, peeled and cut into matchsticks
1 red pepper (capsicum), halved, cored deseeded and
   cut into fine, short slivers
1 fresh hot red chilli, halved, deseeded and finely
   chopped
1 clove garlic, peeled and finely chopped
2 Tbsp peeled and coarsely grated ginger
4 kaffir lime leaves, centre ribs removed, finely
   shredded
juice of 1 lime
2 Tbsp light soy sauce
few drops of sesame oil
3 spring onions, trimmed and chopped
3 Tbsp chopped coriander leaves
50g roasted salted peanuts or cashew nuts,
   chopped, optional

1 Put noodles in a saucepan of gently boiling salted water and cook for 5 minutes. Drain and refresh with cold water until the noodles feel cold. Leave them to drain.

2 If prawns are frozen, thaw them quickly in a sealed plastic bag immersed in a sink of warm water. Twist off their heads, then peel off shells, leaving the small piece of shell on the tail intact. Using a small sharp knife slice down the back of each prawn and gently extract the red or black vein. Rinse prawns and pat dry with paper towels.

3 Heat a wok over high heat then add the oil. When the oil is nice and hot add beans, carrot and red pepper. Stir-fry for 2 minutes, then add chilli, garlic and ginger, then the prawns. Stir-fry for 2 minutes, until prawns change colour.

Stir in lime leaves, lime juice, soy sauce, sesame oil, spring onions and coriander and finally the noodles. Stir-fry until piping hot.

4 Dish into bowls and scatter nuts on top, if using. Serve immediately.

tabbouleh with panfried chicken tenderloins

SERVES 6
TIME TO PREP 15 MINUTES, PLUS 30 MINUTES
  SOAKING TIME FOR BURGHUL
TIME TO COOK 7–10 MINUTES

IT'S EASY TO OVERCOOK SMALL PIECES OF CHICKEN, ESPECIALLY IF THE HEAT IS TOO FIERCE, AS THEY DON'T CONTAIN MUCH FAT AND CAN QUICKLY DRY OUT. COOK THEM UNTIL THE PINKNESS IN THE CENTRE HAS JUST GONE, AND SERVE THEM HOT AND JUICY.

175g (1 cup) fine burghul
2½ cups boiling water
1½ cups finely chopped flat-leaf parsley
1 cup tightly packed mint leaves, chopped
3 spring onions, trimmed and very finely chopped
3 large vine tomatoes, quartered, cored, seeds
**   flicked out, diced**
100ml lemon juice
100ml extra virgin olive oil
salt and freshly ground black pepper
500g chicken tenderloins
1 Tbsp olive oil, plus extra for hot plate

1 Put the burghul in a fine sieve and rinse under running water. Transfer it to a bowl and pour on boiling water. Leave to soak for 30 minutes. Drain well. Transfer to a large serving bowl and add parsley, mint, spring onions and tomatoes.

2 In a bowl whisk together the lemon juice, extra virgin olive oil, 1 teaspoon of salt and a good grinding of black pepper. Pour dressing over the burghul and toss well.

3 Toss chicken tenderloins in 1 tablespoon of olive oil and cook on a preheated lightly oiled barbecue hot plate over medium heat, turning often, until browned all over and just cooked through. Alternatively, heat olive oil in a medium-sized frying pan over medium heat. When the oil is hot, add the chicken tenderloins and cook until golden, turn them over and cook briefly until they are just cooked through; they'll continue cooking as they stand. Season lightly with salt and pepper.

4 Pile tabbouleh into small bowls and arrange the hot chicken pieces on top. Pour any juices from the chicken over and serve immediately.

food over flames

Seared, flamed or singed and cooked over a grill or on a

griddle: scrumptiously good meat and fish dishes that will

rock your taste buds.

tuna steaks with tuna fish mayonnaise

SERVES 4
TIME TO PREP 15 MINUTES
TIME TO COOK 3 MINUTES

ON A SUMMER'S EVE, WITH A GENTLE ZEPHYR BREEZE DANCING OVER YOUR SKIN AND SEA SPRAY IN THE AIR, YOU COULD WANT FOR NOTHING MORE THAN A CHILLED CHARDONNAY AND A PLATTER OF TUNA!

TUNA MAYONNAISE

1 x 185g can tuna in oil, drained
4 anchovy fillets packed in oil, drained
1 rounded Tbsp capers, drained
2 Tbsp lemon juice
½ cup ready-made mayonnaise (use a premium brand made with egg yolks)
salt

TUNA STEAKS

500g piece tuna loin (choose a piece of an even thickness so that it will cook evenly)
1 tsp freshly ground lemon pepper (or the very finely grated zest of 1 lemon mixed with 1 tsp freshly ground black pepper)
1 Tbsp olive oil, plus extra for hot plate
1 Tbsp chopped parsley

1 To make the tuna mayonnaise, put tuna, anchovies, capers and lemon juice in a food processor or blender (liquidiser) and process to combine. Add mayonnaise and mix together. The anchovies will probably provide all the salt you need, but taste and add a few pinches of salt if necessary.

2 To prepare the steaks, roll tuna loin in lemon pepper. Cook the tuna on a preheated oiled barbecue hot plate over medium heat just to sear, about 1 minute each side depending on the thickness of the loin. Be careful; overcooked tuna is dry and boring. Turn the tuna with tongs and make sure all of the outside, apart from the ends, is seared. Alternatively, heat a non-stick frying pan over medium–high heat. Add olive oil, and when the pan is nice and hot, lower in the tuna and cook as described. Transfer tuna to a board and let it cool.

3 When ready to serve, slice the tuna thinly, arrange on a platter and sprinkle with parsley. Serve with tuna mayonnaise sprinkled with parsley.

chicken breasts on the barbie with tomato salsa

SERVES 4
TIME TO PREP 12 MINUTES
TIME TO COOK 15 MINUTES

THE TRICK WITH CHICKEN BREASTS IS TO COOK WHAT USED TO BE THE SKIN SIDE OVER A
HEAT ROBUST ENOUGH TO GIVE THEM GOOD COLOUR AND FLAVOUR, THEN LOWER THE
HEAT A LITTLE AND TURN THE PIECES OVER. THIS ENSURES EVEN COOKING THROUGHOUT.
TRY THE SALSA WITH BARBECUED FISH OR FREE-RANGE PORK CUTLETS, TOO.

1 Put chicken breasts in a shallow dish and pour olive oil over them. Grind over a little black pepper and add thyme sprigs. Cover with plastic food wrap and refrigerate until ready to cook. Bring chicken breasts to room temperature before cooking.

2 Barbecue chicken breasts on a preheated oiled barbecue hot plate over medium heat until a good golden colour and cooked through. The chicken breasts should sizzle along nicely, but don't let the heat get too hot or they will dry out and the flesh will turn stringy. Alternatively, cook chicken breasts in a little hot oil over medium heat in a ridged grill pan. Season with salt and transfer chicken to a plate.

3 Meanwhile, to make the salsa, make sure the tomatoes are well drained and then mix with the garlic, parsley, extra virgin olive oil, capers and lemon juice. Season with salt and plenty of pepper. Spoon salsa over the chicken and serve immediately.

**4 free-range skinned and boned
chicken breasts, rinsed and
patted dry
2 Tbsp olive oil, plus extra for
hot plate
salt and freshly ground black
pepper
8 sprigs thyme**

FRESH TOMATO SALSA
**2 medium-sized vine tomatoes,
diced and drained
2 cloves garlic, peeled and finely
chopped
2 Tbsp coarsely chopped flat-leaf
parsley
2 Tbsp extra virgin olive oil
1½ Tbsp capers, drained
1 Tbsp lemon juice
¼ tsp salt
freshly ground black pepper**

barbecued fish on crushed jersey bennes

SERVES 6
TIME TO PREP 25 MINUTES
TIME TO COOK 25 MINUTES

THIS IS A CLASSY DISH BEST SUITED TO SPRING WHEN FRESHLY DUG POTATOES ARE AVAILABLE. MY PREFERENCE IS FOR MONKFISH, BUT ANY DELICATE WHITE FISH, SUCH AS BLUENOSE OR SNAPPER, WILL WORK.

800g jersey bennes or new season freshly dug potatoes, scrubbed
4 Tbsp butter, softened
1 clove garlic, peeled and crushed
2 Tbsp snipped chives
2 Tbsp chopped flat-leaf parsley
2 Tbsp olive oil
finely grated zest of 1 lemon
sea salt and freshly ground black pepper
750g skinned and boned monkfish fillets, rinsed and patted dry
1 bunch spring onions, trimmed and chopped

1 Cook potatoes in gently boiling salted water until tender, or steam them.

2 Mix butter with garlic, chives and most of the parsley in a small bowl and set aside.

3 Put oil on a plate with lemon zest and a good grinding of black pepper. Pass fish fillets through oil coating both sides. Cook them on a preheated barbecue hot plate over medium heat until golden and nearly cooked through, then turn and cook the other side for 30 seconds, just to sear. Transfer fish fillets to a plate.

4 Meanwhile, drain potatoes and turn them onto a large platter. Crush roughly with a fork and mix in spring onions and garlic and herb butter. Season with plenty of sea salt and freshly ground black pepper and gently mix together. Transfer fish to top of potatoes, sprinkle with a little more sea salt and reserved parsley and serve.

pork balls

SERVES 8 (MAKES ABOUT 40)
TIME TO PREP 20 MINUTES
TIME TO COOK 15 MINUTES

THESE ARE JUST THE THING WHEN YOU WANT A SUBSTANTIAL NIBBLE – WATCH THEM DISAPPEAR! IF YOU DON'T HAVE FRESH BREADCRUMBS, USE A SLIGHTLY SMALLER AMOUNT OF PANKO CRUMBS (AS THEY ARE A LITTLE DRIER). SERVE PORK BALLS HOT, WRAPPED IN LETTUCE LEAVES, WITH A SMATTERING OF FRESH HERBS, SLICED CHILLI AND A DRIBBLE OF SWEET CHILLI SAUCE.

1 stalk lemon grass
650g minced free-range pork
finely grated zest of 1 lime
2 Tbsp fish sauce
2 cloves garlic, peeled and crushed
small knob of fresh ginger, peeled and grated
1 fresh medium–hot red chilli, halved, deseeded and finely chopped
¼ tsp salt
½ cup soft white breadcrumbs
1 large (size 7) free-range egg, lightly beaten
canola or peanut oil for hot plate

Go to www.juliebiuso.com for a video clip of Julie demonstrating this recipe.

1 Smash lemon grass with a mallet and extract the tender part. Chop finely.

2 Put minced pork in a bowl with lemon grass, lime zest, fish sauce, garlic, ginger, chilli, salt, breadcrumbs and egg. Squelch together; I wear disposable food gloves to do this. Shape into 40 small balls and put them in a shallow container as they are done. Cover and refrigerate until ready to cook. Bring to room temperature before cooking.

3 Cook pork balls on a preheated lightly oiled barbecue hot plate over medium heat until golden and cooked through; turn often with two spoons to avoid charring and if the hot plate becomes dry, spray with a little oil. Alternatively, cook the meatballs in hot oil in a large frying pan as described; you may need to do this in batches. Serve hot as soon as they are all done.

lamb cutlets with grilled red peppers

SERVES 6
TIME TO PREP 15 MINUTES
TIME TO COOK 15 MINUTES

GRILLED PEPPERS ADD PLENTY OF FLAVOUR TO SALADS, AND ARE ALSO GOOD AS A TOPPING FOR BRUSCHETTA OR PANINI. BARBECUE A BATCH OF THEM, THEN PEEL, HALVE AND DESEED AS DESCRIBED IN THE RECIPE, TRANSFER THEM TO A CONTAINER, DRIZZLE WITH EXTRA VIRGIN OLIVE OIL AND COVER WITH A LID. THEY'LL KEEP FOR 3–4 DAYS IN THE REFRIGERATOR.

2 red peppers (capsicums)
2 large anchovy fillets packed in olive oil
1 Tbsp extra virgin olive oil
1 large clove garlic, peeled and chopped
1 tsp finely chopped marjoram
1 tiny dried bird's eye chilli, crushed
24 small well-trimmed lamb cutlets
3 Tbsp olive oil, plus extra for hot plate
¼ tsp freshly ground black pepper
salt
2 Tbsp finely chopped flat-leaf parsley
1 tsp red wine vinegar

1 Grill whole peppers over a gas flame, or on a barbecue grill rack, until charred. Transfer to a plate, drape with a paper towel and leave to cool. Peel off blackened skin, remove cores and seeds and dice flesh; reserve all the juices.

2 Mash anchovies to a paste in a small frying pan over a very gentle heat with the extra virgin olive oil, garlic, marjoram and chilli; this can be prepared an hour or so in advance.

3 Put lamb in a dish and pour over olive oil. Grind on pepper. Cook for a few minutes each side on a preheated lightly oiled barbecue hot plate over medium–high heat. Don't overcook; the cutlets should be nice and pink inside. Transfer cutlets to a plate and sprinkle them with salt. Drain briefly before serving. Alternatively, cook cutlets in batches in a little oil in a hot ridged grill pan over medium heat.

4 When the cutlets are nearly done, gently reheat the anchovy mixture; don't let the anchovies fry or they will stiffen. Stir in parsley, vinegar and red pepper juices.

5 Put peppers on a serving plate and arrange cutlets around or on top, spoon over dressing and serve.

barbecued lamb tacos

SERVES 4 (MAKES 8)
TIME TO PREP 15 MINUTES, PLUS 30 MINUTES
  MARINATING
TIME TO COOK 10 MINUTES

THIS IS A GREAT DISH FOR THE KIDS TO MAKE – IT'S NOT
COMPLICATED AND THEY'LL FEEL QUITE PROUD OF THEMSELVES
FOR ACHIEVING IT! FOR A CHANGE, MAKE THE TACOS A HOME FOR
LEFTOVER ROASTED CHICKEN OR CRISP RASHERS OF BACON.

1 Tbsp chilli powder
½ tsp ground cumin
3 cloves garlic, peeled and crushed
finely grated zest of 1 orange
juice of ½ an orange
2 x 200g lamb backstraps
olive oil for hot plate
salt
8 taco shells (or tortillas)
1 x 400g can refried beans, heated,
   or 1 cup hummus, optional
handful of baby salad leaves
1–2 ripe tomatoes, diced
1 cup coriander sprigs
3 spring onions, trimmed and thinly sliced
50g creamy feta, mopped dry and crumbled

1 Mix together chilli powder, cumin, garlic, orange zest
  and juice in a dish. Add lamb and coat with the paste.
Cover and marinate for 30 minutes at room temperature.

2 Scrape the marinade off the lamb, but don't discard it.
  Cook the lamb on a preheated lightly oiled barbecue
hot plate over medium heat for about 3 minutes, then turn
lamb over. Spoon half the reserved marinade on top of the
lamb. Cook a further 2–3 minutes; the lamb should still feel
supple and slightly springy, but not bouncy which indicates it
is rare. Turn lamb again and cook 30 seconds more to cook
the marinade, quickly spooning the rest of the marinade
on top. Finally, turn it one more time to cook through the
last application of marinade. This may sound fiddly, but it's
actually quite straightforward and it is essential because
marinade that has had raw meat in it is not safe to eat unless
it, too, has been cooked.

3 Transfer lamb to a board, sprinkle generously with salt
  and leave to cool. Slice cooled lamb thinly.

4 To serve, warm the taco shells or tortillas for 1–2
  minutes in a warm oven preheated to 120°C. If using
refried beans or hummus, spread a little over the taco shells
and fill with salad leaves, sliced lamb, tomatoes, coriander,
spring onions and feta, in that order. Serve immediately.

meatballs wrapped in lemon leaves

SERVES 6 OR MORE (MAKES ABOUT 40)
TIME TO PREP 25 MINUTES, PLUS AT LEAST 1 HOUR
  CHILLING
TIME TO COOK 12 MINUTES

LEMON LEAVES ADD A GOOD CITRUS FLAVOUR TO THESE
MEATBALLS BUT, LIKE BAY LEAVES, THEY ARE THERE FOR THE
FLAVOUR AND SHOULD BE DISCARDED AFTER COOKING. SERVE
THE MEATBALLS HOT ON THEIR OWN AS A NIBBLE, AS PART OF
A BARBECUE MEAL, OR INSIDE PITA POCKETS WITH A GARLICKY
YOGHURT DRESSING AND SALAD LEAVES.

1 small onion, peeled and finely chopped
50g butter
3 Tbsp water
1¾ fresh white breadcrumbs
90ml milk
250g minced free-range pork
250g minced veal
2 Tbsp finely chopped flat-leaf parsley
1 tsp finely chopped lemon thyme or thyme
1 Tbsp finely chopped marjoram
1¼ tsp salt
freshly ground black pepper
¼ tsp freshly grated nutmeg
1 large (size 7) free-range egg, lightly beaten
olive oil for hot plate

40 fresh unblemished lemon leaves
toothpicks

1 Put onion, butter and 1 tablespoon of water in a saucepan over low heat. Cover and cook gently for 10 minutes. Remove lid and leave to cool.

2 Put crumbs in a large bowl and mix in the milk with a fork. Leave to soften for about 15 minutes.

3 When the onion is cool, add to the crumbs with 2 tablespoons of water, pork, veal, herbs, salt, a good grind of pepper, nutmeg and egg. Mix with a wooden spoon to begin with, then squelch together with your hands; I wear disposable gloves to do this. Shape into balls with wet hands, putting balls on a plate as they are done. Cover and refrigerate for at least 1 hour to firm.

4 Wrap a washed and dried lemon leaf around each meatball securing the leaves with toothpicks. Cook meatballs on a preheated lightly oiled barbecue hot plate over gentle heat, positioning them leaf-side down to begin with. Anoint with a little oil from time to time. Turn with tongs and brown as much meat surface on each meatball as possible. Serve hottish.

fish cakes with cucumber relish

SERVES 6 (MAKES ABOUT 16 CAKES)
TIME TO PREP 20 MINUTES, PLUS 30 MINUTES
  MACERATING
TIME TO COOK 10 MINUTES

THESE FISH CAKES ARE A GOOD HOME FOR LEFTOVER BARBECUED FISH, PREFERABLY A TYPE THAT FLAKES EASILY.

FISH CAKES
750g skinned and boned white fish fillets, rinsed and patted dry
olive oil
¼ cup canned coconut cream
¾ cup fresh breadcrumbs (or a little more if necessary)
½ tsp salt
1 tsp raw sugar
2 Tbsp finely chopped coriander leaves

1 medium (size 6) free-range egg, lightly beaten
2 Tbsp standard white flour, plus extra for dusting cakes

CUCUMBER RELISH
2 Tbsp caster sugar
¼ tsp salt
100ml white vinegar
1 small telegraph cucumber
1 very small red onion, peeled and sliced
1 fresh hot red chilli, halved, deseeded and finely sliced
2 Tbsp chopped coriander leaves

1 Smear fish fillets on both sides with oil. Cook on a preheated lightly oiled barbecue hot plate over medium heat until three-quarters cooked, turning once carefully with a fish slice. Alternatively, cook in a non-stick frying pan. Cool fish briefly then flake with a fork and place in a bowl with coconut cream, breadcrumbs, salt, sugar, coriander and egg. Beat together and shape into fish cakes. Arrange them in a single layer on a plate, cover and refrigerate until ready to cook.

2 To make the cucumber relish, put the sugar, salt and vinegar in a medium-sized bowl and stir until the sugar dissolves. Peel the cucumber, slice lengthways, scoop out seeds with a pointed teaspoon, and slice flesh into half moons. Add to bowl along with onion, chilli and coriander. Stir together and leave to macerate for 30 minutes before serving.

3 Dust fish cakes lightly with flour and shake off the excess. Cook fish cakes on a preheated well oiled barbecue hot plate over low–medium heat, brushing or spraying with a little oil from time to time, until golden on both sides. Alternatively, heat a little olive oil in a large frying pan over medium heat and fry fish cakes on both sides until golden. Drain briefly on paper towels and serve hot with cucumber relish.

pork chops with lychees and micro salad

SERVES 4
TIME TO PREP 30 MINUTES, PLUS 30 MINUTES MARINATING
TIME TO COOK 10 MINUTES

PORK CHOPS GO WITH APPLE SAUCE, SO WHY NOT LYCHEES? IT'S A COMBINATION THAT
HAS BEEN POPULAR IN CHINESE COOKING FOR A VERY LONG TIME WITH GOOD REASON!

2 Tbsp safflower or light vegetable oil, plus extra for hot plate

1 stem lemon grass, smashed with a mallet

1 fresh hot red chilli, halved, deseeded and chopped

2 kaffir lime leaves, centre ribs removed, finely shredded

4 free-range pork chops or cutlets

1 x 560g can lychees, drained, juice reserved

salt

MICRO SALAD

1½ cups very fresh bean sprouts, trimmed

2 cups (about 50g) micro cress or baby greens with edible flower petals

½ cup fresh mint leaves, shredded

½ cup coriander leaves

2 kaffir lime leaves, centre ribs removed, finely shredded

1 Tbsp fish sauce

2 Tbsp lime juice

1 Tbsp lychee juice reserved from can

¼ cup toasted salted peanuts, finely chopped, optional

1 Choose a dish large enough to hold the chops and put in 2 tablespoons of oil with the lemon grass, chilli and shredded lime leaves. Add pork chops and turn them to coat in the marinade. Cover and marinate at room temperature for 30 minutes.

2 To prepare the salad, put the bean sprouts, micro cress or baby greens, mint, coriander and shredded lime leaves in a bowl and toss lightly together. Mix fish sauce, lime juice and lychee juice together in a small bowl.

3 Cook chops on a preheated oiled barbecue hot plate over medium heat for 3–5 minutes a side until nearly cooked through. Spoon extra marinade on to keep them sizzling as they cook. Don't overcook; the chops should still have a pink tinge if cut open. If cooked until they are white inside they will be tough and dry; they will continue to cook as they rest. Alternatively, heat 1 tablespoon oil in a large frying pan over medium heat and cook as described.

4 Towards the end of the cooking time, add lychees to the barbecue hot plate and cook for a few minutes. Transfer chops to a plate when they're done and season with salt. Spoon the lychees on the side or top.

5 Quickly mix dressing through salad, sprinkle peanuts on top, if using, and serve with hot pork chops and lychees.

tuna fish cakes

SERVES 4 (MAKES 12)
TIME TO PREP 25 MINUTES
TIME TO COOK 10 MINUTES

SERVE WITH SAUCE TARTARE, MAYONNAISE OR THICK YOGHURT
FLAVOURED WITH CRUSHED GARLIC AND CHOPPED MINT, AND A
ROCKET SALAD WITH TANGY VINAIGRETTE.

1 x 400g can white beans, such as cannellini,
   drained, rinsed and drained
2 x 185g cans tuna in oil, drained
bunch of spring onions, trimmed and chopped
finely grated zest of 1 lemon
1 Tbsp chopped flat-leaf parsley
1 small (size 5) free-range egg, lightly beaten
¼ tsp salt
freshly ground black pepper to taste
¼ cup panko or dried breadcrumbs
1½ Tbsp olive oil for hot plate
1½ Tbsp butter for hot plate

1 Tip beans onto paper towels and pat dry. Mash beans
in a bowl with a potato masher, leaving them a little
lumpy. Add tuna, spring onions, lemon zest, parsley, beaten
egg and salt and pepper. Shape tuna mixture into 12 cakes.
If not for immediate use, put tuna cakes on a plate, cover
and refrigerate.

2 Tip crumbs onto paper towels and roll the tuna cakes in
them one by one. Cook on a preheated oiled barbecue
hot plate over medium heat, adding little pats of butter from
time to time to keep the tuna cakes sizzling. Cook on both
sides until golden. Alternatively, heat oil in a frying pan over
medium heat and add butter. Once butter is sizzling, add
tuna cakes and cook on all sides until golden. Serve hot with
sauce of your choice.

pork patties with fennel seeds and lemon

SERVES 4–6 (MAKES 16)
TIME TO PREP 20 MINUTES
TIME TO COOK 20 MINUTES

SERVE THESE PATTIES WITH CHUTNEY AND SALAD.

1 medium-sized onion, peeled
1 clove garlic, peeled and crushed
1 Tbsp butter
900g minced free-range pork
finely grated zest of 1 lemon
½ tsp fennel seeds
1 medium (size 6) free-range egg yolk
2 Tbsp tomato ketchup
1 tsp salt
¼ tsp freshly ground black pepper
olive oil for hot plate

1 Cut onion in half. Finely chop one half of the onion. Put
chopped onion, garlic and butter in a small saucepan
over medium heat. Cover with a lid and cook gently until
softened but not coloured. Transfer to a large bowl, cover
and cool.

2 Add pork, lemon zest, fennel seeds, egg yolk, tomato
ketchup, salt and pepper to the cooled onions and
squelch together; I wear disposable food gloves to do this.
Shape into 16 patties. Cover and refrigerate until ready to
cook. Bring patties to room temperature about 15 minutes
before cooking.

3 Cook patties on a preheated oiled barbecue hot plate
over medium heat until golden and cooked through.
Transfer them to a plate as they are done; you'll probably
need to do this in 2 batches.

4 Slice the other half of the onion. As you turn the last
batch of patties over to cook the second side, add the
sliced onion to the plate and cook until the onion is golden.
Dish the second batch of patties and onion onto the plate,
drain briefly, then transfer everything to a heated serving
plate. Alternatively, cook the patties and onion in a little hot
oil in a frying pan over medium heat, removing onions to a
side plate once they are coloured. Serve hot.

indonesian chicken cakes with tomato chilli sauce

SERVES 4 (MAKES 24)
TIME TO PREP 25 MINUTES, PLUS AT LEAST 1 HOUR
  CHILLING
TIME TO COOK 20 MINUTES

SERVE THESE CAKES HOT WITH TOMATO CHILLI SAUCE, WEDGES OF
LIME AND LEMON, THICKLY SLICED CHUNKS OF CUCUMBER AND
FINELY SLICED RED CHILLI ON THE SIDE. THE SPICY TOMATO SAUCE
IS EXCELLENT WITH OTHER MEATS AS WELL AS FISH, BUT IT'S AT ITS
BEST USED WITHIN 24 HOURS OF MAKING.

CHICKEN CAKES

**1 Tbsp canola or peanut oil for frying, plus extra for
  hot plate**
2–3 medium-sized shallots, thinly sliced (about ½ cup)
1 large clove garlic, peeled and chopped
½ tsp salt
freshly ground black pepper
**500g free-range skinned and boned chicken
  breasts, cubed**
2 medium (size 6) free-range eggs
2 Tbsp cornflour

TOMATO CHILLI SAUCE

**2–3 medium-sized shallots, sliced (should yield about
  ½ cup sliced shallots)**
2 Tbsp kecap manis
1 large tomato, peeled, deseeded and chopped
2 Tbsp water
1 Tbsp lime juice
1 tsp sliced fresh hot red chilli
½ tsp sugar
½ tsp salt

1 To make the chicken cakes, heat oil in a large frying pan. Add shallots and garlic and fry for 5–7 minutes, until lightly golden and sweet-smelling. Stir in salt and plenty of black pepper.

2 Put cubed chicken in a food processor and process to a coarse paste. Add eggs, cornflour and shallot mixture. Process until just combined. Shape mixture into small flat cakes and put them on a plate lined with baking paper.

Cover and refrigerate for at least 1 hour until firm; they can be prepared several hours ahead but bring to room temperature before cooking.

3 To make the sauce, process all the ingredients together until smooth. Cover and chill until ready to serve.

4 Cook chicken cakes on a preheated oiled barbecue hot plate over medium heat until golden. Don't attempt to move the chicken cakes until they are well browned or they will stick and tear; once the protein cooks, they will be easy to move around on the hot plate. Turn them over and cook the other side until golden. Alternatively, heat a little oil in a large frying pan over medium heat and fry chicken cakes on both sides until golden. Drain briefly on paper towels. Serve with tomato chilli sauce.

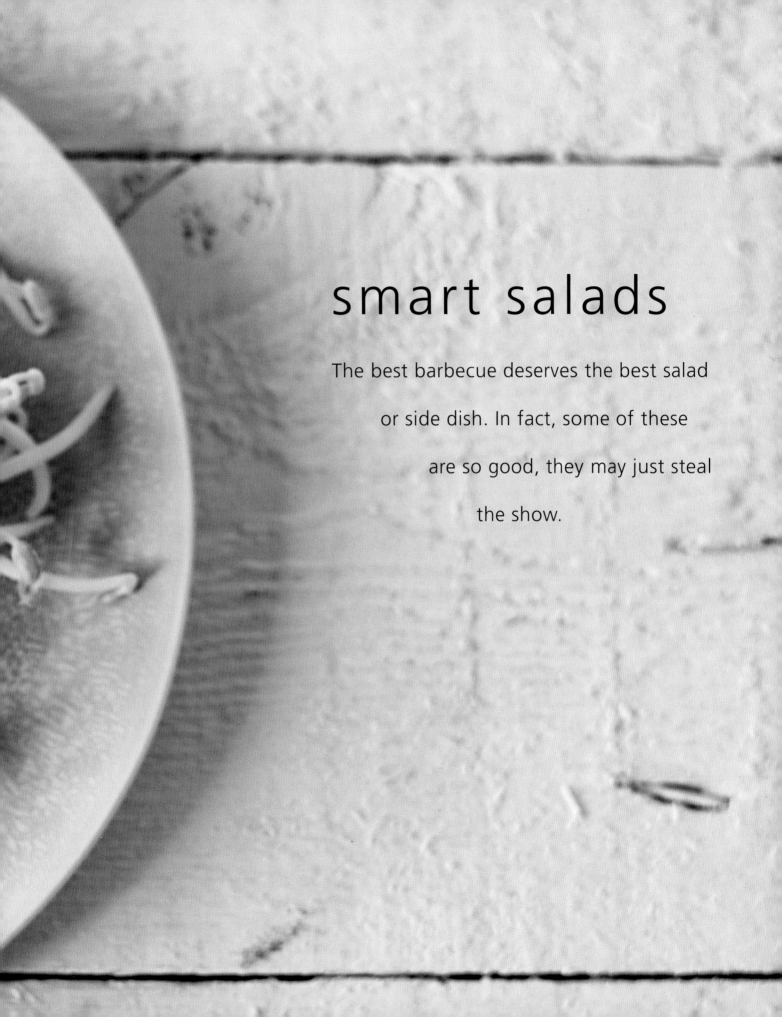

smart salads

The best barbecue deserves the best salad

or side dish. In fact, some of these

are so good, they may just steal

the show.

tomato and mint salad

SERVES 6
TIME TO PREP 10 MINUTES, PLUS 15 MINUTES FOR
   SOAKING ONION
TIME TO COOK NONE

THE TRICK WITH THIS SALAD IS TO USE SWEET VINE TOMATOES OF DIFFERENT SIZES AND COLOURS. ONE GREEN TOMATO IN THE SALAD CAN ADD A TOUCH OF PLEASANT ACIDITY.

½ small red onion, peeled and cut into slivers
2 cups cherry tomatoes
4–6 assorted vine tomatoes
1 cup loosely packed mint leaves
sea salt and freshly ground black pepper
3 Tbsp lemon-infused extra virgin olive oil

1 Soak slivered onion in icy cold water for 15 minutes. Drain and pat dry with paper towels.

2 Halve the cherry tomatoes and cut the larger tomatoes into wedges or thick rounds, cutting out cores. Put tomatoes in a shallow bowl or on a deep platter. Scatter with mint and red onion and grind on plenty of pepper. Just before serving, drizzle with oil and sprinkle with sea salt. Serve immediately.

beach-side salad

SERVES 4 OR MORE
TIME TO PREP 15 MINUTES
TIME TO COOK NONE

CLEAN FRESH FLAVOURS ARE THE HALLMARK OF THIS SALAD – IT'S JUST THE THING TO GO WITH BARBECUED SEAFOOD AND MEATS.

12–16 smallish vine tomatoes
1 Tbsp lemon juice
sea salt and freshly ground black pepper
½ small telegraph cucumber
¼ cup kalamata olives, drained, or sun-dried
   Greek olives
150g feta, mopped dry and crumbled
1 Tbsp dried Greek or Sicilian oregano, crumbled
2–3 Tbsp extra virgin olive oil for drizzling

1 Slice tomatoes any way you fancy and leave them to drain for 5 minutes. Pour off the liquid. Put tomatoes on a flat serving dish and drizzle with lemon juice. Season with sea salt and black pepper.

2 Peel cucumber and cut into thick slices, then into small chunks. Add these and the olives to the dish.

3 Mound crumbled feta in the centre of the dish and scatter the oregano over everything. Drizzle with oil and serve immediately.

fattoush

SERVES 4
TIME TO PREP 20 MINUTES
TIME TO COOK NONE

BREAD IS A GREAT ADDITION TO A SALAD, ESPECIALLY IF IT'S CRUNCHY. IT MAY NOT BE AUTHENTIC TO TOAST THE BREAD FOR THIS LEBANESE SALAD, BUT IT TASTES SO MUCH NICER! EXTEND THE SALAD BY ADDING CANNED OR BARBECUED FRESH TUNA OR OTHER BARBECUED FISH OR CHICKEN FILLETS.

1 small red onion, peeled and sliced
2 large pita breads
3 Tbsp olive oil
½ telegraph cucumber, peeled and chopped, or 2 Lebanese cucumbers, chopped
2 radishes, trimmed and sliced
1 medium-sized carrot, peeled and sliced
1 white stalk celery, well washed and sliced
1 small cos lettuce or 120g cos lettuce leaves, washed, dried and torn into bite-sized pieces
2 Tbsp chopped mint
2 Tbsp chopped flat-leaf parsley
12 ripe cherry tomatoes, halved

DRESSING
2 cloves garlic, peeled and crushed
2 Tbsp lemon juice
1 tsp sumac
5 Tbsp extra virgin olive oil
¾ tsp salt
¼ tsp freshly ground black pepper
¼ tsp allspice

Go to www.juliebiuso.com for a video clip of Julie demonstrating this recipe.

1 Soak red onion in icy cold water for 15 minutes. Drain and pat dry with paper towels.

2 Split pita breads open and brush both sides with oil. Put them on a tray and bake in an oven preheated to 180°C for 5–7 minutes until golden.

3 Put red onion in a large bowl with cucumber, radishes, carrot, celery, cos lettuce, herbs and tomatoes.

4 To make the dressing, put all the ingredients in a small bowl and mix together. Pour over salad and toss thoroughly. Break pita bread into bite-sized pieces and add to salad. Toss lightly and serve immediately.

barbecued pepper and feta salad

SERVES 6
TIME TO PREP 15 MINUTES
TIME TO COOK 12 MINUTES

THIS IS A CLASSIC COMBINATION, BUT ONE THAT WORKS SO WELL ON EVERY LEVEL. VISUALLY, IT'S BRIGHT AND SUMMERY, IT SMELLS REALLY GOOD AND TASTES DIVINE. MAKE A MEAL OF IT WITH CRUSTY BREAD – THERE'RE HEAPS OF JUICES TO DUNK THE BREAD INTO – OR SERVE IT AS AN ACCOMPANIMENT TO BARBECUED MEATS.

4 red peppers (capsicums)
4 yellow peppers (capsicums)
3 Tbsp extra virgin olive oil
¼–½ tsp salt
1½ Tbsp lemon juice
freshly ground black pepper to taste
½ cup basil leaves
150g creamy feta cheese, mopped dry and
   thinly sliced

1 Cook peppers on a barbecue grill rack over high heat, turning often until charred. Alternatively, cook them over a gas flame. Transfer peppers to a plate, drape with paper towels and leave to cool. Remove blackened skin, core, seeds and membranes from peppers. Don't wash the peppers or you will lose valuable flavour; simply rinse your fingers from time to time when they get sticky. Cut flesh into fat strips. Reserve any juices. The peppers can be prepared a day ahead. Cover and refrigerate, but bring to room temperature before serving.

2 Put peppers in a bowl with any juices and pour over the oil. Add ¼ teaspoon of salt and lemon juice. Grind on black pepper then give everything a good toss. Taste and, if necessary, add a little more salt; how much you need will depend on the saltiness of the feta.

3 Just before serving, add the basil and stir it through the peppers. Transfer to a serving dish and arrange feta on top. Spoon some of the juices on top of the feta and serve immediately.

barbecued asparagus

SERVES 4
TIME TO PREP 15 MINUTES
TIME TO COOK 7–10 MINUTES

TOWARDS THE END OF THE SEASON ASPARAGUS SPEARS ARE A LITTLE LESS SUCCULENT. DOUSING THEM WITH OIL AND COOKING THEM ON THE BARBECUE KEEPS THEM NICE AND JUICY AND MAKES THEM TASTE GREAT.

16 plump asparagus spears
2 Tbsp avocado oil, plus a little extra for drizzling
1 tsp marjoram leaves
2 cloves garlic, peeled and crushed
salt and freshly ground black pepper
½ cup freshly grated parmesan cheese
100g soft fresh goat's cheese, sliced
½ cup semi-dried tomatoes, drained and sliced
basil leaves for garnishing
8 thin slices ciabatta bread, dried out in the oven
   until crisp

1 Trim asparagus, rinse well and pat dry. Put avocado oil in a shallow dish with marjoram and garlic and season with salt and a good grinding of black pepper. Put asparagus spears in seasoned oil and roll them around until well-coated.

2 Cook asparagus spears on a preheated barbecue hot plate over medium heat until caramelised. Scoop garlicky bits that fall from the spears to one side and transfer to a plate as they brown.

3 Divide asparagus spears among 4 plates and scatter with parmesan and garlicky bits. Top with 1–2 slices of goat's cheese and a few slices of semi-dried tomatoes. Drizzle with avocado oil, grind on some pepper and garnish with basil leaves. Serve immediately with baked ciabatta.

salad of green beans, rocket and feta

SERVES 4
TIME TO PREP 12 MINUTES
TIME TO COOK 5 MINUTES

THE TEXTURE OF THE BEANS IS ALL-IMPORTANT IN THIS SALAD. IF THEY ARE REALLY CRUNCHY THEY WILL NOT MELD WITH THE OTHER INGREDIENTS AND YOU'LL END UP WITH MOUTHFUL AFTER MOUTHFUL OF ALMOST-RAW BEANS TO MASTICATE.

450g slim green beans, or snow beans, trimmed
salt and freshly ground black pepper
3 Tbsp extra virgin olive oil
1 Tbsp white wine vinegar
1 clove garlic, peeled and crushed
1 Tbsp creamy Dijonnaise mustard
¾ cup cherry tomatoes, halved
130g rocket, trimmed
150g feta, drained, mopped dry and crumbled

1 Plunge beans into a saucepan of gently boiling salted water and cook for several minutes, until they just start to soften. Drain immediately and refresh with plenty of cold water. Leave beans to drain, then pat dry with paper towels. Transfer beans to a bowl.

2 Mix oil, vinegar, garlic, mustard, half a teaspoon of salt and plenty of black pepper together in a small bowl and pour dressing over the beans. Toss well. Add cherry tomatoes, toss carefully, then add rocket leaves and toss again. Transfer to a shallow platter, scatter feta on top and serve immediately.

aubergine and white bean salad

SERVES 6 OR MORE
TIME TO PREP 20 MINUTES
TIME TO COOK 10–15 MINUTES

THIS IS A GOOD, RELIABLE BEAN SALAD WITH A BIT MORE INTEREST THAN MOST. AUBERGINE, TOMATOES, BASIL AND A TANGY MUSTARDY DRESSING GIVE IT HEAPS OF FLAVOUR.

2 large aubergines (eggplants)
olive oil
sea salt
4 Tbsp extra virgin olive oil
2 Tbsp lemon juice
1 Tbsp creamy Dijonnaise mustard
1 clove garlic, peeled and crushed
2 Tbsp chopped flat-leaf parsley
salt and freshly ground black pepper
2 x 400g cans white beans, drained, rinsed
** and drained**
250g cherry tomatoes, halved
½ cup basil leaves

1 Cut aubergines lengthways into long thin slices. Put a little olive oil on a large plate and dunk slices one at a time in the oil, letting excess oil drip off. Transfer them to a barbecue grill rack heated to medium; you'll need to move the slices around often as they cook to prevent scorching. Cook quickly until tender and golden and lightly charred around the edges. Transfer aubergine slices to a clean plate as they are done and season them with sea salt. Repeat with remaining aubergine slices. Alternatively, cook aubergine slices in a ridged grill pan heated to medium–high.

2 Mix extra virgin olive oil, lemon juice, mustard, garlic, parsley, half a teaspoon of salt and plenty of black pepper in a large bowl. Add the white beans and toss well.

3 Slice tomatoes in half and leave to drain for 5 minutes. Gently stir the tomatoes, aubergine and basil leaves through the bean salad and serve immediately.

kachumbar

SERVES 6
TIME TO PREP 20 MINUTES, PLUS 1 HOUR DRAINING
TIME TO COOK NONE

THIS SHARP AND PUNGENT SALAD REALLY LIVENS UP GRILLED
MEATS AND FISH. IT'S ALSO GOOD WITH INDIAN DISHES.

2 medium-sized white or red onions, peeled
salt
1 Tbsp tamarind pulp
½ cup hot water
1 Tbsp brown sugar
4 large vine tomatoes, skinned and diced
2 fresh hot green chillies, halved, deseeded and
    finely chopped
1 Tbsp roughly chopped mint leaves
2 Tbsp roughly chopped coriander leaves
2 Tbsp coarsely peeled and grated ginger

1 Slice the onions very thinly, put them in a sieve resting
over a bowl and sprinkle with salt. Leave them to drain
for 1 hour, then rinse thoroughly under cold running water.
Pat onions thoroughly dry with paper towels then put them
in a bowl.

2 Put tamarind pulp in a small bowl and pour in hot water.
Leave to soften for 5 minutes, then use your fingers to
separate the pulp from the seeds. Push the mixture through
a sieve and discard seeds and tough fibre.

3 Mix brown sugar and sieved tamarind. Put onions,
tomatoes, chillies, mint and coriander in a bowl and
pour the tamarind liquid over them. Squeeze in the juice
from the grated ginger, sprinkle with half a teaspoon of salt
and stir thoroughly. Cover and chill before serving.

barbecued sweet corn salad with semi-dried tomatoes and avocado

SERVES 4–6
TIME TO PREP 25 MINUTES
TIME TO COOK 35 MINUTES

SERVE THIS SALAD WITH BARBECUED FISH, CHICKEN OR TURKEY,
OR GET SOME WRAPS AND ROLL IT UP. YOU COULD ALSO ADD
SOME SIZZLED HAM OR BACON TO GIVE IT A BIT MORE PUNCH.

4 sweet corn cobs
2 Tbsp lime juice
2 Tbsp extra virgin olive oil or avocado oil
sea salt and freshly ground black pepper
2 cloves garlic, peeled and crushed
2 Tbsp chopped coriander leaves
1 ripe but firm avocado
12 semi-dried tomatoes, halved

1 First, remove the silks from the corn cobs. Pull down
the husks leaf by leaf, remove the silks, then rewrap the
cobs with the husks carefully. Bind them with string; don't
use nylon string or it will melt. Soak corn cobs in cold water
for 15–30 minutes. Cook corn cobs over hot coals for 15–30
minutes, turning often. If you don't have hot coals at your
disposal, cook the corn cobs on a preheated lightly oiled
barbecue hot plate over medium heat. Splash the corn cobs
with cold water from time to time to create steam, and turn
them every few minutes. If the barbecue has a lid, cook the
cobs mostly with the lid down; they'll take 25–35 minutes to
cook. Remove from heat and leave to cool.

2 When corn cobs have cooled enough to handle, remove
husks and slice off kernels. Put corn kernels in a large
bowl. Pour most of the lime juice and all the oil over the
corn kernels and half a teaspoon of sea salt and a little black
pepper. Add garlic and coriander and stir well.

3 Halve avocado, remove stone and peel. Cut into cubes
or slices and sprinkle with remaining lime juice. Season
with salt and pepper. Put avocado and tomatoes on top of
the corn salad. Mix together gently and serve immediately.

orange and red onion salad

SERVES 4–6
TIME TO PREP 25 MINUTES
TIME TO COOK NONE

THIS SALAD IS REALLY REFRESHING AND CAN BE SERVED AS PART OF A TAPAS SELECTION WITH HAM, SEAFOOD OR CHICKEN. IT'S ALSO GOOD MADE WITH TANGELOS INSTEAD OF ORANGES.

1 small red onion, peeled
4 juicy oranges
2 Tbsp avocado oil
1 Tbsp lemon juice
½ tsp salt
freshly ground black pepper
1 clove garlic, peeled and finely chopped
1 tsp chopped marjoram
⅓ cup roughly chopped flat-leafed parsley leaves
125g feta, mopped dry and cubed
½ cup large green olives, drained

1 Cut onion in half then into fine slivers. Soak in icy cold water for 15 minutes. Drain and pat dry with a paper towel.

2 Peel oranges with a serrated knife, taking care to remove all the white pith. Cut orange flesh into rounds and put the slices in a bowl with all the juices.

3 Mix avocado oil, lemon juice, salt, a good grinding of black pepper, garlic, marjoram and parsley together in a large bowl. Add feta, olives and onion. Toss well. Add orange slices, but not the juice; you can drink that! Toss again and serve immediately. Alternatively, layer the ingredients in a glass bowl and pour the dressing over.

sauces, salsas, dips and dunks

A spoonful here, a little drizzle there – these accompaniments

add interest to all kinds of food as they unleash

explosions of full-on flavour.

roasted tomato sauce with honey and cinnamon

SERVES 6
TIME TO PREP 15 MINUTES
TIME TO COOK 7 MINUTES

THIS SAUCE IS QUITE BEGUILING – I THINK IT'S THE SWEET SPICE OF CINNAMON COMBINED
WITH SCENTED GRUNTY HONEY AND THAT LITTLE BACK-KICK OF CHILLI WHICH DOES IT.
IT WORKS WELL WITH CHICKEN BURGERS, FREE-RANGE PORK AND LAMB CUTLETS AND
THE LIKE.

1 Grill the tomatoes over a preheated hot barbecue grill rack until the skins blacken and split. Alternatively, cook them in the flames of a gas element or under a hot oven grill; spear 2–3 tomatoes at a time onto a long-handled metal skewer, and turn them with tongs as they char. Transfer tomatoes to a plate when they are done and leave them to cool.

2 Heat oil in a smallish frying pan over medium–high heat. Add the bread slices and cook on both sides until golden. Remove bread to a side plate. Pound the bread in a mortar and pestle with the salt, then work in the garlic, cinnamon, paprika, chilli powder and lemon zest and pound until smooth. Work in the lemon juice and honey.

3 Remove skins from tomatoes. Squeeze tomato flesh through your fingers into a bowl, forming a rough purée; discard any tough cores. Press the tomato purée through a coarse sieve, to remove the seeds. Mix in the pounded bread and seasonings. Taste and adjust seasoning; add a little more salt or lemon juice, if required. Cover with plastic food wrap and refrigerate. Bring to room temperature and garnish with lemon peel before serving.

10 medium-sized vine tomatoes
2 Tbsp olive oil
3 slices sourdough bread
½ tsp salt
1 clove garlic, peeled
½ tsp ground cinnamon
¼ tsp smoked Spanish paprika (sweet)
¼ tsp chilli powder
finely grated zest of 1 lemon
1 Tbsp lemon juice
1½ Tbsp manuka or scented honey
finely sliced lemon peel for garnishing

muhammara

SERVES 8
TIME TO PREP 15 MINUTES
TIME TO COOK 20 MINUTES

THIS SYRIAN WALNUT AND ROASTED RED PEPPER DIP IS UTTERLY
DELICIOUS. SERVE IT AS A DIP WITH HOT PUFFY PITA BREADS AT
THE START OF A BARBECUE GATHERING, OR TO ACCOMPANY
BARBECUED CHICKEN OR LAMB DISHES.

150g fresh walnut halves
3 large red peppers (capsicums)
1–2 thick slices (60g) ciabatta bread
2 cloves garlic, peeled and crushed
1 fresh hot red chilli, halved, deseeded and finely
  chopped
1½ Tbsp pomegranate molasses, plus extra
  for drizzling
1 tsp salt
finely grated zest of 1 lemon
1½ Tbsp lemon juice
60ml extra virgin olive oil
1 Tbsp chopped flat-leaf parsley
1 Tbsp chopped mint leaves, plus extra leaves
  for garnishing
lemon wedges for garnishing
sliced fresh red chilli for garnishing
warmed pita bread for serving

Go to www.juliebiuso.com for a video clip of Julie
demonstrating this recipe.

1 Spread walnut halves in a shallow ovenproof dish and
roast in an oven preheated to 180°C for 7–10 minutes
until lightly browned. When the walnuts are cool, roughly
crumble them with your fingers and take them out to the
garden and blow off any loose skins; walnut skins taste
bitter.

2 Cook whole peppers on a barbecue grill rack over high
heat, turning often until charred. Alternatively, cook them
over a gas flame. Transfer peppers to a plate, drape with
paper towels and leave to cool. Remove blackened skin, core,
seeds and membranes from peppers. Don't wash the peppers
or you will lose valuable flavour; simply rinse your fingers
from time to time when they get sticky. Cut flesh into strips.

3 Remove and discard crusts from bread. Cut bread
into cubes and put in a food processor and process
to form breadcrumbs. Add peppers, walnuts, garlic, chilli,
pomegranate molasses, salt, lemon zest and juice and
process until pasty, then trickle the oil in through the feed
tube while the machine is running to form a purée.

4 Transfer purée to a bowl, add chopped parsley and mint
and stir through. Serve garnished with lemon wedges, a
drizzle of pomegranate molasses, a smattering of mint and
chilli and warmed pita bread on the side.

spicy chilli dressing

SERVES 4–6
TIME TO PREP 5 MINUTES, PLUS 2–3 HOURS TO RIPEN
TIME TO COOK NONE

SERVE THIS AT THE BEGINNING OF A BARBECUE AS A DIPPING
SAUCE WITH A SELECTION OF FRUIT ARRANGED ON A PLATTER.
I LIKE TO INCLUDE SLICED MANGO, PAWPAW, BANANA, PINEAPPLE,
CUBES OF AVOCADO, SEGMENTS OF PINK GRAPEFRUIT AND
CANNED LYCHEES.

1–2 fresh hot red chillies, halved, deseeded and
  finely chopped
2 Tbsp kecap manis or dark soy sauce
100g palm sugar, finely shaved with a sharp knife, or
  dark muscovado sugar
4 Tbsp lemon juice

1 Put all ingredients in a small bowl and stir until sugar
is dissolved. Leave dressing to ripen for 2–3 hours,
stirring occasionally, until it is clear. Taste and adjust the
heat by adding more chilli, if preferred. Serve dressing in a
bowl for dipping or pour it over a platter of fruit and serve
immediately with plenty of paper serviettes.

fresh tomato salsa

SERVES 4
TIME TO PREP 12 MINUTES
TIME TO COOK NONE

A FRESH SALSA SHOULD BE SERVED THE DAY OF MAKING. THIS ONE IS GOOD WITH FISH, LAMB, PORK, CHICKEN AND EVEN HAMBURGERS AND FRIES.

8 small vine tomatoes, halved and
   cores removed
1 Tbsp lemon juice
¼ tsp sugar
1 Tbsp extra virgin olive oil
1½ Tbsp chopped coriander leaves
1 large clove garlic, peeled and crushed
¼ tsp Tabasco Sauce
¼ tsp salt
2 spring onions, trimmed and finely chopped

1 Finely dice tomatoes and transfer to a sieve placed over a bowl. Leave to drain for 10 minutes.

2 Mix lemon juice, sugar, oil, coriander, garlic, Tabasco Sauce, salt and spring onions together in a bowl, add drained tomatoes and gently stir together. Transfer to a serving dish.

smoky tomato salsa

SERVES 6
TIME TO PREP 10 MINUTES
TIME TO COOK 7 MINUTES

THIS IS GREAT WITH FREE-RANGE PORK CUTLETS AND A WHITE BEAN SALAD. IT KEEPS IN THE REFRIGERATOR FOR 2–3 DAYS SO LEFTOVERS, IF THERE ARE ANY, AREN'T A PROBLEM!

4 large vine tomatoes
2 fresh hot red chillies
3 spring onions, white part only, finely chopped
2 Tbsp chopped coriander leaves
½ tsp sea salt
finely grated zest of 1 lime
1 Tbsp lime juice

1 Grill the tomatoes over a preheated hot barbecue grill rack until the skins blacken and split. Alternatively, cook them in the flames of a gas element or under a hot oven grill; spear 2–3 tomatoes at a time onto a long-handled metal skewer, and turn them with tongs as they char. Transfer tomatoes to a plate when they are done and leave them to cool.

2 Remove skins, cut open, discard seeds and chop flesh finely. Put in a bowl with chillies, spring onions and coriander. Season with sea salt and stir in lime zest and juice. Cover with plastic food wrap and refrigerate until required. Bring to room temperature before serving.

coriander and coconut chutney

SERVES 6
TIME TO PREP 12 MINUTES
TIME TO COOK NONE

SWEET AND PUNGENT AND GOOD WITH BARBECUED WHITE FISH, CHICKEN AND LAMB DISHES, THIS CHUTNEY KEEPS FRESH FOR ABOUT A WEEK.

1 tightly packed cup (about 2 large bunches) coriander
1 Tbsp raw sugar
1 tsp salt
2 Tbsp desiccated coconut
1 Tbsp peeled and coarsely grated ginger
2 fresh hot green chillies, halved, deseeded and roughly chopped
1 medium-sized onion, peeled and roughly chopped
2 Tbsp lemon juice

1 Wash coriander, shake off excess water, then pat dry with paper towels. Chop coarsely.

2 Put all ingredients in the bowl of a food processor or blender (liquidiser) and process until finely chopped. Transfer to a container, cover and chill until required.

mango salsa

SERVES 4–6
TIME TO PREP 15 MINUTES
TIME TO COOK NONE

THIS FRESH AND JUICY SALSA CAN BE MADE WITH UNRIPE MANGOES, IF PREFERRED – IT'LL BE LESS SWEET BUT MORE CRUNCHY. SERVE WITH BARBECUED FREE-RANGE PORK CHOPS OR CHICKEN BREASTS, WHOLE BARBECUED FISH OR BUTTERFLIED LEG OF LAMB. THE SALSA IS AT ITS BEST FRESHLY MADE, OR UP TO 30 MINUTES AFTER MAKING.

1 tsp caster sugar
2 Tbsp lime juice
1–2 mangoes, perfectly ripe but not squishy
1 clove garlic, peeled and finely chopped
1 tsp finely grated ginger
bunch of spring onions, white part only, finely chopped
1 fresh hot red chilli, halved, deseeded and finely chopped
½ tsp salt
1 tsp sesame oil
2 Tbsp chopped coriander leaves

1 Put sugar and lime juice in a small ramekin and stir until sugar dissolves. Peel mangoes and cut the flesh away from the stone. Sprinkle lime juice and sugar over mango pieces and toss gently.

2 Add garlic, ginger, spring onions, chilli, salt and sesame oil and toss gently. Just before serving, add coriander and stir through.

spicy satay sauce

SERVES 6
TIME TO PREP 12 MINUTES
TIME TO COOK 20 MINUTES

THIS IS GREAT WITH ANY SATAYED MEAT WITH CHUNKS
OF CUCUMBER AND RED ONION ON THE SIDE. IT KEEPS IN THE
REFRIGERATOR FOR UP TO 3 DAYS BUT IS BEST SERVED AT
ROOM TEMPERATURE OR WARM.

¼ cup peanut oil
1 onion, peeled and finely chopped
2 large cloves garlic, peeled and crushed
4 tiny dried bird's eye chillies, crushed
small knob of fresh ginger, peeled and roughly
  chopped
175g roasted, shelled peanuts
3 Tbsp kecap manis, plus extra for drizzling
1 Tbsp brown sugar
¾ cup hot water, or more, to thin

1 Heat oil in a frying pan over a gentle heat. Add onion
and fry for about 15 minutes until soft and a pale gold
colour.

2 Add garlic, chillies and ginger and cook for a few
minutes more. Transfer mixture to a food processor or
blender (liquidiser) and add peanuts, kecap manis, brown
sugar and ¼ cup of hot water. Process until smooth;
add more hot water to bring it to a good dipping-sauce
consistency. Cover and and refrigerate until required. Before
serving, drizzle a little kecap manis on top.

chilli dipping sauce

SERVES 4–6
TIME TO PREP 7 MINUTES
TIME TO COOK NONE

A HANDY DIPPING SAUCE TO SERVE WITH BARBECUED PRAWNS,
SQUID, PORK BALLS OR CHICKEN AND PORK SATAY.

2 large cloves garlic, peeled and finely chopped
2 Tbsp lime juice
2 Tbsp fish sauce
1 Tbsp brown sugar
2 fresh hot red chillies, finely chopped
¼ cup water

1 Put all ingredients in a small bowl and stir until sugar is
dissolved. Taste and adjust seasoning, if required; add
more lime juice to sharpen, more sugar to sweeten, more
fish sauce if it tastes flat and more chilli to make it hotter.

golden kiwifruit salsa

SERVES 6–8
TIME TO PREP 15 MINUTES, PLUS 30 MINUTES
  MARINATING
TIME TO COOK NONE

THIS QUICKLY MADE FRESH SALSA GOES WELL WITH CHICKEN,
PORK AND DUCK DISHES.

1 Tbsp liquid honey
juice of 1 lime
2 fresh hot red chillies, halved, deseeded and very
  finely chopped
2 Tbsp shredded lemon or lime basil or mint
6 golden kiwifruit, peeled and finely chopped

1 Mix the honey, lime juice, chillies and basil or mint in a
bowl and add the golden kiwifruit. Stir together gently
and marinate for 30 minutes before serving.

shallot vinaigrette

SERVES 4
TIME TO PREP 7 MINUTES
TIME TO COOK NONE

THIS DRESSING GOES WELL WITH ROBUST SALAD LEAVES,
SUCH AS COS AND ICEBERG LETTUCE, RADICCHIO AND SPINACH,
AND WITH COOKED VEGETABLES, SUCH AS GREEN BEANS,
CAULIFLOWER, CARROTS AND BEETROOT. USE IT WITHIN
1–2 HOURS OF MAKING FOR BEST EFFECT.

6 Tbsp extra virgin olive oil
2 Tbsp red wine vinegar
2 Tbsp finely chopped shallots
2 tsp creamy Dijonnaise mustard
1 Tbsp thyme leaves
1 tsp sea salt
freshly ground black pepper, to taste

1 Put all ingredients, including a good grinding of pepper, in a small bowl and whisk together. Cover and refrigerate until required.

mango honey salsa

SERVES 4
TIME TO PREP 10 MINUTES
TIME TO COOK NONE

SWEET, SHARP AND HOT – THIS SALSA GIVES BARBECUED
CHICKEN, PORK AND LAMB DISHES AN INTERESTING JAB!
IF MANGO IS UNAVAILABLE, USE A PAWPAW INSTEAD.

½ tsp manuka or scented honey
¼ tsp salt
2 Tbsp lemon juice
1 fresh hot red chilli, deseeded and finely chopped
2 Tbsp chopped coriander leaves
1 Tbsp chopped mint
1 perfectly ripe mango

1 Put honey, salt and lemon juice in a bowl and stir until honey dissolves. Add chilli, coriander and mint and stir through.

2 Peel mango, cut the flesh away from the stone and cut into small cubes. Toss gently with dressing. Cover and refrigerate for up to 1 hour before using; it will keep longer, but it is at its best when freshly made.

cucumber mayonnaise dip

SERVES 6
TIME TO PREP 7 MINUTES
TIME TO COOK NONE

A QUICKLY MADE SUMMERY DIP THAT ALSO SERVES AS A
DRESSING – THIS IS GREAT WITH SEAFOOD, SUCH AS SQUID,
PRAWNS AND CRAYFISH.

**1 cup ready-made mayonnaise (choose a premium
  brand made with egg yolks)**
1 Tbsp lemon juice
2 cloves garlic, peeled and crushed
**½ small telegraph cucumber, peeled, halved,
  deseeded and diced**
1 Tbsp chopped mint

1 Mix the mayonnaise with the lemon juice and garlic. Stir
in cucumber and mint. Cover and chill until required.

cucumber and pineapple sambal

SERVES 6–8
TIME TO PREP 15 MINUTES
TIME TO COOK NONE

JUICY, SWEET, SOUR AND SPICY – THIS SAMBAL IS JUST THE RIGHT
FOIL FOR SPICY FOOD OR TO JAZZ UP BARBECUED LAMB, CHICKEN
OR FISH.

½ large telegraph cucumber
½ fresh pineapple, peeled and diced
1 medium-sized red onion, peeled and thinly sliced
1 fresh hot red chilli, finely sliced
½ tsp salt
2 Tbsp sugar
3 Tbsp lime juice
**2 kaffir lime leaves, centre ribs removed, finely
  shredded, optional**

1 Peel cucumber, cut in half lengthways and scoop out
the seeds with a pointed teaspoon, then slice thickly.
Put cucumber in a bowl with pineapple, red onion, chilli,
salt, sugar, lime juice and lime leaves, if using, and mix
thoroughly. Cover and chill until ready to serve.

sweet endings

Too hard to resist! Fresh, fruity, smooth,

chilling and thrilling, with the emphasis on fast: sweet

mouthfuls to savour at the end of an outdoor feast.

lemon and elderflower granita

SERVES 8
TIME TO PREP 15 MINUTES
TIME TO COOK 5 MINUTES
TIME TO FREEZE 1–2 HOURS

THERE'S NOTHING BETTER THAN A CHILLED GLASS OF FLUFFY FLAVOURED ICE (THAT'S
GRANITA) TO CONCLUDE A BARBECUE ON A HOT DAY. ELDERFLOWER SYRUP HAS A MUSKY,
FLORAL SCENT WHICH ADDS COMPLEXITY TO LEMON GRANITA. IF IT'S UNAVAILABLE, USE
LIMONCELLO INSTEAD.

¾ cup sugar
pared rind of 6 lemons
1 litre cold water
20 mint leaves, washed
**125ml strained lemon juice (about
    4 tart lemons)**
4 Tbsp elderflower syrup

1 Place sugar in a pan with lemon rind and water over gentle heat until sugar dissolves; stir occasionally. When the sugar is dissolved bring syrup to the boil, removing any scum from the surface. Boil briskly for 5 minutes.

2 Take pan off the heat and add mint leaves and lemon juice. Leave mixture to infuse for 15 minutes, then strain into a shallow glass or china dish. Stir through elderflower syrup. Leave to cool.

3 Place in freezer and allow to partially freeze; this will take 1–2 hours. Remove granita from freezer and break any frozen pieces into flakes with a fork. Return granita to the freezer and repeat the process, breaking up any ice crystals and returning it to the freezer several times until the granita has the consistency of fluffy ice. Serve in chilled glasses. Alternatively, cover granita with plastic food wrap and return it to the freezer until required; it will keep for up to 6 weeks.

quick strawberry trifles

SERVES 4
TIME TO PREP 20 MINUTES, PLUS 15–20 MINUTES
  STEEPING TIME FOR STRAWBERRIES
TIME TO COOK NONE

THERE'S LITTLE POINT IN MAKING YOUR OWN SPONGE FOR THESE
TRIFLES AS IT GETS SQUISHED AND SQUASHED IN THE GLASSES;
I BUY MINE FRESHLY MADE BY THE SUPERMARKET! DON'T LEAVE
OUT THE GROG – IT MAKES THEM!

**2 punnets (about 500g) strawberries, hulled and sliced
  (should yield 3 cups sliced strawberries)**
3 Tbsp caster sugar
200ml cream
finely grated zest of 1 lemon
1 Tbsp lemon juice
150g trifle sponge, or light egg sponge cake, cubed
**4 Tbsp Cointreau, Grand Marnier, dry sherry or
  orange juice**
¼ cup slivered almonds, toasted

1 Put the strawberries in a bowl with 2 tablespoons
caster sugar. Mix carefully then cover and leave at room
temperature for 15–20 minutes, until the juices run.

2 Whip the cream with 1 tablespoon sugar until it is
holding shape, but don't make it stiff and buttery, then
fold through lemon zest and juice.

3 Assemble trifles in glasses, putting in layers of sponge
splashed with liqueur, sherry, or juice, cream and
strawberries. Finish with cream and strawberries on the top
and sprinkle over a few toasted almonds. Serve immediately
or cover with plastic food wrap and chill for up to 1 hour
before serving.

fresh apricot trifle

SERVES 6
TIME TO PREP 15 MINUTES, PLUS TIME TO COOL
TIME TO COOK 20 MINUTES

THERE'S ALWAYS SOMEONE WHO GRIZZLES ABOUT THE FACT
THAT THERE IS NOT ENOUGH BOOZE IN THE TRIFLE AND SOMEONE
ELSE WHO SAYS THERE'S TOO MUCH! MAKING INDIVIDUAL TRIFLES
SOLVES THAT PROBLEM, AS YOU CAN TAILOR THEM TO PEOPLE'S
TASTES. THIS RECIPE IS ALCOHOL–FREE BUT IF YOU WANT TO
GIVE IT AN ALCOHOLIC LIFT ADD A LITTLE BRANDY TO THE
APRICOT SYRUP.

1 cup sugar
600ml water
**10–12 firm-but-just-ripe apricots, halved and stones
  removed**
150ml cream
100g trifle sponge, or light egg sponge cake, cubed
100ml ready-made crème anglaise
toasted nuts, optional

1 Put the sugar and water in a large frying pan over low
heat until the sugar dissolves. Stir once or twice; do not
let the water boil until the sugar has melted or the syrup
may crystallise later. When dissolved, boil for 2 minutes.
Add apricots, cut side up. Let syrup boil up over the fruit to
seal cut surfaces. Immediately lower heat to lowest setting
and let fruit poach very gently for about 15 minutes or until
tender. Spoon juices over fruit from time to time. Leave
apricots to cool in the syrup. Drain cooled apricots, reserving
syrup.

2 To assemble one large trifle or individual trifles, first
whip cream lightly. Layer cubed sponge, apricots, cream
and crème anglaise, using three-quarters of a cup of the
reserved apricot syrup or half a cup of apricot syrup mixed
with 3 tablespoons of brandy for moistening the sponge
as you go. Sprinkle nuts on top, if using. Serve immediately
or cover with plastic food wrap and chill for up to 1 hour
before serving.

fresh cherry trifle

SERVES 4–6
TIME TO PREP 25 MINUTES
TIME TO COOK NONE

THIS IS DESIGNED FOR FRESH CHERRIES AND THE TIME TO MAKE IT IS MID-SEASON ONCE THE PRICE OF CHERRIES HAS DROPPED, BUT BEFORE THE QUALITY DROPS.

450g fresh cherries
300g trifle sponge, or light egg sponge cake
120ml Frangelico, kirsch or Amaretto
200ml cream
1 Tbsp caster sugar
seeds scraped from ½ vanilla pod
400g ready-made crème anglaise
⅓ cup Valrhona chocolate dots or grated
  dark chocolate

1 Set aside 4–6 perfect cherries for garnishing. Pit the rest of the cherries with a cherry pitter, then cut cherries in half. Alternatively, cut cherries in half and remove stones.

2 Split trifle sponge in half through the middle, cut it into small cubes then put pieces on a plate and sprinkle with chosen liqueur.

3 Lightly whip cream, adding caster sugar and the vanilla seeds.

4 Arrange layers of trifle sponge, cherries, crème anglaise, chocolate and cream in individual serving glasses or a large dessert bowl. Serve immediately, garnished with reserved cherries, or cover and refrigerate for up to 6 hours before serving.

easy coffee semifreddo

SERVES 8
TIME TO PREP 20 MINUTES, PLUS FREEZING TIME
TIME TO COOK NONE

THIS IS A CHEAT'S SEMIFREDDO (THERE'S NO GELATINE USED) BUT THE TEXTURE OF THE LITTLE TURNED-OUT DESSERTS IS VELVETY AND SMOOTH. AND, YES, THEY WOBBLE JUST AS THEY SHOULD (LIKE A YOUNG WOMAN'S BREASTS).

300g mascarpone
400g quark
4 Tbsp icing sugar
1 tsp vanilla extract
50ml Tia Maria or coffee liqueur
chocolate scrolls or flakes for garnishing, optional
hot espresso coffee for serving

Go to www.juliebiuso.com for a video clip of Julie demonstrating this recipe.

1 Beat mascarpone and quark in a bowl with a wooden spoon until combined and smooth. Beat in icing sugar, vanilla extract and liqueur. Spoon into 8 ramekins or moulds and freeze for at least 2 hours; the desserts can be made a day or two in advance but any longer and the mixture goes grainy.

2 Transfer to the refrigerator 1 hour before serving to allow the mixture to soften. To release puddings, dip them one at a time in a sink of hot water for just a second, then quickly run a flat-bladed knife between mould and pudding and turn the pudding onto a plate. Garnish with chocolate scrolls or flakes, if using. Serve with small cups of piping hot espresso coffee for pouring over desserts.

buttermilk hotcakes with raspberries and strawberries

SERVES 6 (MAKES 24)
TIME TO PREP 15 MINUTES
TIME TO COOK 15 MINUTES

HOTCAKES, PANCAKES AND PIKELETS ARE ETERNALLY POPULAR WITH KIDS. THESE ARE QUITE A BIT MORE INVOLVED THAN SIMPLE HOTCAKES WITH MAPLE SYRUP BUT, IF THE KIDS WANT THEM, GET THEM DECKED OUT IN THEIR APRONS, WEIGHING AND SLICING AND LOOKING FORWARD TO A TASTY REWARD!

4 medium (size 6) free-range eggs
2 cups buttermilk
100g butter, melted and cooled but still liquid
2½ cups self-raising flour
4 Tbsp caster sugar
butter for hot plate
500g fresh or frozen raspberries, thawed if frozen
icing sugar
1 punnet (about 250g) strawberries, hulled and sliced
  (should yield 1½ cups sliced strawberries)
Greek yoghurt, ricotta or vanilla ice cream
  for serving
2 Tbsp chopped pistachio nuts for garnishing

CHOCOLATE SAUCE
80g dark chocolate, broken into squares
1 Tbsp butter
½ cup cream
4 Tbsp golden syrup

1 Whisk eggs and buttermilk together in a large bowl, then whisk in cooled butter. Sift flour over the top and sprinkle on the sugar. Whisk again to form a lump-free batter.

2 Drop spoonfuls onto a preheated lightly buttered barbecue hot plate and cook over medium heat. Add batter with a large spoon, spreading it out slightly, leaving enough room for the hotcakes to spread. Cook for 3–4 minutes until the hotcakes are golden brown underneath. Turn hotcakes over with a spatula and cook the other side. Transfer to a plate as they are done and keep warm,

covered with a clean tea towel, while cooking remaining hotcakes. Alternatively, cook in a large non-stick lightly greased frying pan over medium heat in batches of three.

3 Rub raspberries through a sieve and sweeten to taste with two tablespoons of icing sugar. Sprinkle sliced strawberries with a little icing sugar.

4 To make the chocolate sauce, put chocolate in a heatproof bowl, add butter, cream and golden syrup and set bowl over a small pan of hot water. Heat pan gently, stirring chocolate as it melts. Use sauce while it is warm.

5 To assemble the hotcakes, stack 2–3 per serving, and top with a blob of yoghurt, ricotta or ice cream. Spoon strawberries on top, and drizzle with raspberries and warm chocolate sauce. Sprinkle nuts on top and serve immediately.

roasted plums with lavender petals

SERVES 3–6
TIME TO PREP 10 MINUTES
TIME TO COOK 20 MINUTES

DIVINE! SO PRETTY! LOVELY TO EAT! YOU'LL GET LOTS OF BROWNIE POINTS WHEN YOU SERVE THESE.

6 firmish plums or nectarines, halved and stones
  removed
few pinches of fresh lavender petals
12 very small fresh bay leaves
large piece vanilla pod, split open
caster sugar
French vanilla ice cream for serving

1 Put plums in a shallow roasting dish lined with baking paper. Distribute lavender petals and bay leaves amongst them. Scrape vanilla seeds over fruit and sprinkle fruit with caster sugar.

2 Bake for 15–20 minutes in an oven preheated to 220°C (fanbake) until softened and caramelising. Cool fruit briefly and serve with ice cream.

coffee and chocolate cream with raspberries

SERVES 6
TIME TO PREP 15 MINUTES PLUS 1 HOUR CHILLING
TIME TO COOK NONE

THIS IS LIKE TIRAMISU, BUT WITH RASPBERRIES. IF FRESH RASPBERRIES ARE NOT AVAILABLE, USE FROZEN ONES BUT THAW THEM FIRST. THEY'RE USUALLY CONSIDERABLY CHEAPER THAN FRESH RASPBERRIES AND IN THIS RECIPE IT DOESN'T MATTER!

50g dark rich chocolate
½ cup sweetened espresso coffee
3 Tbsp coffee liqueur, such as Tia Maria
200ml cream
seeds scraped from ¼ vanilla pod
2 cups (about 300g) raspberries
100g sponge fingers
200g ready-made crème anglaise

1 Put chocolate in a food processor and process until almost a powder but with a few little chunky nuggets remaining. Reserve a little for garnishing.

2 Mix coffee and coffee liqueur together. Lightly whip cream with vanilla seeds. Reserve a few raspberries for garnishing. Crumble sponge fingers and, splashing the crumbled biscuits with the coffee mixture as you go, layer sponge fingers with cream, crème anglaise, raspberries and chocolate in individual glasses or a large dessert bowl.

3 Dust the top with reserved chocolate and garnish with reserved raspberries. Cover and refrigerate until ready to serve.

fluffy pancakes with maple syrup

SERVES 4–6 (MAKES ABOUT 20 X 8CM PANCAKES)
TIME TO PREP 12 MINUTES
TIME TO COOK 20 MINUTES

THESE ARE WHAT THEY SAY, NICE AND LIGHT AND FLUFFY!

2 cups standard white flour
pinch of salt
1½ tsp baking powder
2 tsp caster sugar
2 large (size 7) free-range eggs
500ml buttermilk
½ tsp vanilla extract
2 Tbsp melted butter, plus extra for hot plate
soft butter, whipped with a wooden spoon,
   for serving
maple syrup for serving

1 Sift flour, salt, baking powder and sugar into a large bowl. Separate eggs; put the whites in a grease-free bowl and the yolks in a jug. Put buttermilk and vanilla extract in the jug with the yolks and whisk together. Add melted butter and whisk again.

2 Beat egg whites until just stiff. Pour buttermilk mixture into dry ingredients and stir until just mixed. Fold in egg whites.

3 Cook pancakes on a preheated lightly buttered barbecue hot plate over gentle heat. Drop tablespoons of mixture onto hot plate and spread mixture a little with a spoon so the pancakes measure about 8cm across. Cook until golden brown. Flip and cook the other side until golden. Transfer to a cake rack and keep warm, covered with a clean tea towel, while cooking remaining hotcakes. Alternatively, cook pancakes in a large non-stick frying pan over medium heat.

4 Serve warm with whipped butter and maple syrup.

berry macaroon creams

SERVES 4
TIME TO PREP 20 MINUTES, PLUS 1 HOUR CHILLING
TIME TO COOK NONE

AN ALTERNATIVE DESSERT CAN BE MADE USING 300G (2 CUPS)
OF STRAWBERRIES WHEN THEY ARE IN SEASON.

finely grated zest of ½ orange, plus a few twists for garnishing
375g (about 3 cups) mixed blueberries and raspberries
3 Tbsp plus 1 tsp orange juice
1 Tbsp kirsch or Cointreau
100g macaroons or almond biscuits, crumbled
1 Tbsp caster sugar
200ml cream
¼ cup coarsely chopped toasted almonds

1 Remove zest from orange and then juice. Place berries in a glass serving bowl and pour on 3 tablespoons of the orange juice and chosen liqueur. Keeping them in fairly big pieces, scatter the macaroons or almond biscuits over the berries and stir gently once or twice to mix them through. Spoon into individual glasses.

2 Put the sugar and 1 teaspoon of orange juice in a small bowl and stir until the sugar dissolves. Add orange zest. Lightly whip cream until it is only just holding shape. Fold in the sugar and orange mixture. Reserve a few berries for the top. Spoon cream over the berries and biscuits. Top with reserved berries, sprinkle nuts on top and add a few twists of orange zest. Cover and chill for up to 1 hour before serving.

gingernut creams with pears

SERVES 4
TIME TO PREP 12 MINUTES, PLUS 1 HOUR CHILLING
TIME TO COOK NONE

THIS DEAD-EASY DESSERT LOOKS POSHER THAN IT REALLY IS BUT
IT'S CHILD'S PLAY, SO GET YOUR KIDS ON TO IT!

175g gingernut biscuits
1 cup cream
1 x 820g can pears, drained and patted dry
½ cup ready-made crème anglaise

1 Put gingernut biscuits in between two layers of paper towels and press on them with a rolling pin to crush them. Keep some larger pieces; don't turn them into powder. Lightly whip the cream, keeping it flowing.

2 Layer up pears, crushed biscuits, crème anglaise and cream in individual glasses in that order. Finish with a little sprinkle of crushed biscuits on top. Cover and refrigerate for at least 1 hour, but up to 4 hours, before serving.

know-how

barbecue tips

When marinating meat, put the meat and marinade in a sturdy, sealable plastic bag and put the bag in a bowl. This makes it easy to turn the meat over when required. The bowl is in case the bag springs a leak!

After skewering meats and vegetables, lay skewers on a clean surface and press gently to make the pieces of meat and vegetable lie flat. This ensures that all the ingredients will have contact with the barbecue hot plate and will cook evenly.

Always have oil on hand. I generally use olive oil, though sometimes canola, peanut or safflower oil for Asian dishes. Oil in a squeezy bottle is convenient, but a large brush with natural bristles or fingers of heatproof silicon – not nylon – and a coffee cup of oil will do. It's better to use a tall container than a bowl so the brush can rest in it without it tipping over.

It's better to use oil rather than butter on a barbecue hot plate to prevent sticking and to create a little sizzle, because it can reach a higher temperature than butter before breaking down. Butter can be used providing the temperature of the hot plate is kept at medium or below medium. Add butter in little dabs, on top of or around the food, during cooking. If you put a great whack of it on at the start, it's likely to burn before the food starts sizzling and oozing a little juice.

Always preheat the barbecue before starting to cook; allow about 10 minutes for a gas barbecue.

Watch the temperature during cooking. While a little charring probably won't hurt, and a touch of caramelisation or bitterness can add interest to a dish, too much blackened food should be avoided. Most food is better cooked on a medium heat or even cooler to begin with. You can always increase the heat towards the end to finish browning. If food, such as chicken, is cooked on too high a heat and quickly blackens, it forms a hard skin and is difficult to cook all the way through to the centre. If this happens, transfer it to an ovenproof dish and finish the cooking in the oven and you may be able to pick off the worst of the charring, too.

Glazes and marinades with sweet ingredients such as honey, brown sugar, fruit juice and syrup easily catch. They're best dabbed on the food towards the end of cooking to increase colouring.

Do not overload the barbecue grill rack or hot plate because it will trap juices around the food, making them steam rather than sizzle. It also makes it difficult to turn over delicate items.

All equipment with pointy prongs should be banned from the barbecue area! Resist the urge to keep on prodding, poking, turning and moving food on a grill rack or hot plate. And never pierce food – you'll let precious juices leak out. Let food settle, let it find its own cooking rhythm. Protein ingredients will often stick at the beginning of cooking and will free themselves nicely once they're cooked. If you forcibly try to turn stuck pieces of meat, you'll tear the fibres and ruin the surface of the meat. Constantly moving food around on the hot plate and grill interferes with the cooking momentum and causes the temperature to drop. Get the temperature right, then just let food do its own thing, cooking along at a nice audible little sizzle, not a fierce fry-up!

Some barbecues have a wok attachment but wok-cooking requires a very high temperature. Cold air or wind will quickly lower the cooking temperature – so, use baking sheets to make a wind shield around the wok and wok attachment. If you cover the sheets with aluminium foil on the side facing the barbecue, you can peel the foil off after cooking and save yourself from a messy clean-up.

It's much easier to clean a gas barbecue while it is still hot. Splash a cup of water onto the hot plate and scrape any residue into the side trough and mop it up with paper towels (steam is hot, so use tongs). Dry off the hot plate with more paper towels. Wait until charcoal barbecues are completely cold before emptying the ash.

For more information on barbecuing, including tips on choosing a barbecue, the difference between wood-fired, charcoal-burning and gas-burning barbecues, and grilling and using a hot plate, tips on cooking meat and fish, and pointers on equipment, safety and health, go to www.juliebiuso.com and select 'Barbecue know-how'.

glossary and food tips

Aïoli

Garlic mayonnaise. It is best made with fresh young garlic if you can get it. Alternatively, remove pale yellow sprouts from more mature garlic.

Asparagus

There is plenty of research to support the inclusion of foods rich in antioxidants in our diet, but it may come as a surprise to learn how high asparagus rates. Watercress tops the antioxidant chart, followed by kumara (sweet potato), and asparagus comes in third. Despite the antioxidant levels dropping by around 50% in canned asparagus, it still beats many fresh vegetables. There's plenty of potassium, good amounts of calcium, and magnesium and phosphorus, too. It's low in salt and has a good amount of fibre. Asparagus has practically no fat, but it does go well with fat – think butter, cream, cheese and olive oil.

Is there a good reason to peel asparagus? There's none that I can think of. However, it does reveal a paler shade of green, and if that takes your fancy, peel away. Otherwise, just trim the ends with a sharp knife or snap them off. Snapping the ends ensures you don't waste any tender part of the asparagus – the spears will only snap where they are tender. Sometimes, though, snapped asparagus spears look shaggy and you have to trim them anyway!

Lemon, verjuice and flavoured vinegars add a fresh taste to asparagus, which is particularly welcome if a dish contains cream or other rich ingredients. Just be aware that these acids can discolour asparagus, so they should be reserved for dishes intended to be served straight away. Always dress asparagus salads just before serving.

Aubergine (eggplant)

You'll often come across an instruction in a recipe to salt aubergine before cooking to draw out bitter juices. It is also often recommended when making pickles and chutneys to remove moisture, ensuring watery juices won't seep out of the aubergine during storage.

Nowadays, however, most varieties of aubergine, especially those grown in hot-houses, do not require salting. Just carry on with the recipe, ignoring that step. Immature aubergines usually have a thin layer of green just under the skin and give off a smell like freshly cut green peppers when sliced or cut – these are best salted before cooking. Old aubergines, on the other hand, can be bitter and are best salted, or not used at all.

The best way to salt aubergines is to slice or cut them as directed in the recipe, then layer them in a colander, sprinkling each layer with salt. Put a plate under the colander and let them drain for 30 minutes. Pat slices dry with paper towels and continue according to the recipe.

Producing deep golden slices of fried aubergine with crispy skin, unctuous creamy flesh and rich flavour is easy when you know how. Contrary to popular belief, most of us don't use enough oil. The key point is: the more oil you use and the hotter it is, the less of it the aubergine will absorb. I learnt this from my Sicilian mother-in-law, who really was a superb cook and she had no fear of hot oil. That's the secret – if slices of aubergine sit in a little oil on a medium heat they go SLURP, sucking up the oil like a thirsty sponge! And if oil is too shallow it loses heat each time more aubergine is added. So, have the oil at least 5 centimetres deep and as hot as you dare and watch what happens when you lower in a few slices of aubergine – they'll repel the oil and bubble and brown in a matter of minutes.

I often cook slices of aubergine in a wok, adding a few slices at a time, making sure they do not overlap and that the oil doesn't stop bubbling. After frying, I transfer the slices to a cake rack with a tray underneath so any excess oil can drip off. I then gently mop the drained slices with paper towels.

Water and oil don't mix – if the aubergine slices are wet they'll spit like crazy when they're lowered into the oil. It's important to mop the slices dry with paper towels before frying. I use olive oil for frying but you can use any oil that has a high flash-point – that means it can get nice and hot before it starts to break down.

I find one of the best ways to cook aubergine is on a barbecue hot plate. Brush each slice with oil – don't be mean with it or the aubergine will dry out – and cook both sides until a rich golden brown. Cooked this way, aubergine has an incomparable flavour with a hint of smoke. It can be cooked directly on a barbecue grill, but it'll need constant turning to prevent burning.

To cook aubergines with the least amount of oil possible, bake them in the oven. Brush slices on both sides with oil and spread them on a baking tray lined with baking paper. Bake for 30–40 minutes in a hot oven, turning once or twice with tongs, until golden brown. This is an excellent method when using it in pies or layered pasta dishes where excess oil could make the dish too rich.

One last point I've got to mention is the furry carpet syndrome! Aubergine is astringent and if it is undercooked it can cause a nasty mouth-puckering sensation that leaves you feeling as if you've sucked on a lemon. Before you know it, your tongue and palate feel furry – just as if you've licked the carpet! My advice is to overcook, rather than undercook, aubergine. That way, it'll develop much more flavour, too.

Avocado oil and avocados
Avocado oil, like the fruit, is rich in monounsaturated fatty acids and a good source of vitamin E. In a nutshell, monounsaturated fatty acids lower bad cholesterol and increase good cholesterol and vitamin E is an antioxidant that protects cells in the body and helps them defend against life-threatening diseases.

Avocado oil gets its striking emerald green colour from chlorophyll and, like the best olive oils, it has a good thick consistency. It feels smooth in the mouth but not fatty – there's no astringency, no acidity, no burning, no peppery bite. You could say it tastes like globe artichokes, maybe, followed by a pronounced lingering flavour of avocado. At 255°C, it has a high smoke point and it breaks up around 268°C. This makes it suitable for quick searing of food when you need very hot oil.

It heightens the flavour of any dish featuring avocado and it complements all kinds of seafood. But, don't think of avocado oil as a replacement for extra virgin olive oil. Rather, think of it as something different – a new flavour to introduce instead of other oils, or blend it with olive oil. The benefits of avocado oil outweigh those of extra virgin olive oil, but its use is more limited.

And here's a tip: to stop avocado halves wobbling around on serving plates, slice a small piece off the outside curve of each half to provide a stable base.

Bacon
Bacon is the name for pork which has been preserved or cured in dry salt, a salt solution, or brine. Sugars or syrups are sometimes added to the cure for extra flavour. After curing, bacon is sold as unsmoked bacon, also known as green bacon. Bacon is also smoked for extra flavour. Traditionally, the skin – called the rind – is left on, but rindless bacon is becoming more popular.

A side of bacon, which is half a pig cut lengthways, provides different cuts of bacon, coming from the shoulder, belly and back. Sliced bacon is usually taken from the middle and belly and the meaty legs provide joints and steaks, or are turned into hams.

Shoulder bacon, the cheapest, can be sliced into rashers, or chopped to use in pies and quiches or other dishes calling for chopped bacon, or it can be cut into joints for boiling. At its best it is a good meaty cut and at its worst it is full of water and impossible to fry.

Middle bacon is the premium cut, taken from the loin (called the eye of the loin)with a strip of belly meat (called the tail). It's the most popular breakfast bacon.

Streaky bacon is taken from the belly of the pig and produces stretchy slices which are the type to go for when lining terrines or wrapping around the likes of asparagus or prunes before barbecuing or grilling. It crisps well in the pan or under the grill and has a sweeter flavour than the other cuts. Bacon hocks and bones are used for stocks and soups.

My preference for all pork products, including bacon, is that they come from free-range pigs.

When buying vacuum-packed bacon: check that it is not swimming in liquid or overly moist – if it is, it will not fry well. Look for dry bacon with creamy fat and rosy meat. Store bacon in its packaging until ready to use, but once a packet is opened, transfer any unused bacon to a clean container, refrigerate and use within 5 days.

Baking powder and bicarbonate of soda
Baking powder is a mix of a mild acid, usually cream of tartar, and a mild alkali, usually bicarbonate of soda, that forms a chemical reaction when wetted. The effervescing is caused by carbon dioxide forming and the gas causes baking to rise.

Bicarbonate of soda is more commonly known as baking soda.

Balsamic vinegar
This superior vinegar, a specialty of Modena in Italy, is made using a

centuries-old technique: the juice of trebbiano grapes is boiled down to a syrup, then poured into wooden barrels where it is left for at least five years, but in some cases much longer. The resulting vinegar is aromatic, spicy and sweet-sour to taste. It should be used sparingly.

The adage 'you get what you pay for' certainly applies to balsamic vinegar. Aceto Balsamico Tradizionale, sold in small squat bottles with long necks, is the numero uno of balsamics. It has a hefty price tag, too, of course, but a few drops will impart an explosion of flavour that cannot be faked. Most cheap balsamic vinegars sold in supermarkets contain caramel, not grape syrup and, although they're fine for liberally splashing around salads and vegetables and into marinades, they do not even come close to the real thing.

Banana leaves
Washed and dried banana leaves can be used as plates for serving grilled food. With the central ribs removed, the leaves can be shaped into cones and used as food containers by first passing the banana leaves over a flame to soften them and make them flexible, or by blanching them in boiling water for a few seconds. The softened leaves can also be used as wrappers for fish, vegetables and meats.

When making banana-leaf parcels: buy freshly picked, supple, pale-green leaves without tears and use natural string to tie the parcels together.

Bird's eye chillies
These tiny pointed chillies are moderately hot with sweet fruity plummy notes. They provide a tingle on the tongue when used in moderation, but an explosive fiery heat when used

generously. I've used them often throughout this book and they are widely available in dried form. Use whole or crushed, as directed. For nutrition information see Chillies, on page 168.

Bread
A baguette, also known as French bread or a French stick, is a long, thin stick of crusty bread.

Ciabatta are slipper-shaped, flattish loaves of bread with a holey texture, a distinctive sour taste and a thin, chewy crust. It is Italian in origin. Use ciabatta fresh, rebaked until crisp or to make bruschetta.

Sourdough breads made with natural or 'wild' yeasts take their name from the characteristic flavour they develop during their lengthy fermentation – they have a distinctive acid tang. They generally have a strong crust and chewy texture and are good keepers. This is real bread!

Bruschetta
The name bruschetta has its origin in the Italian verb *bruscare*, which means to roast over coals. It possibly dates back to Roman times, where slices of crusty bread were cooked over coals and drizzled with newly pressed oil and served to peasants and farm workers after the olive harvest. Bruschetta is now used to describe grilled bread with a range of toppings. The bread is classically rubbed with garlic and drizzled with oil after grilling. The bruschetta recipes in this book are the fancy-pants versions, like gourmet sandwiches, but don't forget the original bruschetta in warmer weather – it's hard to beat good bread grilled over hot coals, rubbed with fresh garlic, drizzled with freshly-pressed extra

virgin olive oil and seasoned with a little sea salt. Devour it around the barbecue with a whiff of smoke in the air. More substantial bruschetta can be served as filling snacks or as light meals and are better served on a plate than in the fingers.

Burghul
Burghul is hulled wheat that has been partially cooked by steaming, then dried and ground. Although the outer layers of bran are removed, the inner layers are kept intact making burghul an extremely nutritious food. It contains B1 niacin, phosphorus, iron and copper, and is a good source of complex carbohydrate. Before using, rinse burghul well. To use in salads, soak in water to cover then drain thoroughly, patting dry with paper towels. Burghul can be steamed or boiled and served hot. Use coarsely ground burghul to stuff vegetables or chicken and finely ground burghul for salads, such as tabbouleh.

Look for organically grown burghul in specialist food shops; buy it in small quantities, store it airtight, and use it within about a month of purchase.

Buttermilk
The term buttermilk was originally used to describe the liquid residue of milk or cream after it was churned to make butter. These days 'cultured' buttermilk is made by adding a natural culture to standard milk or skimmed milk. Using buttermilk for baking – think scones and hotcakes – makes it lighter and adds a pleasant, slightly tangy flavour.

Here's how to make a good substitute for buttermilk: add a few squirts of lemon juice to milk and leave it at room temperature for 30 minutes – it won't have quite the full nutty-sour taste of

buttermilk but it'll be very close.

Cabbage
Cabbage is always available and as cheap as chips, but most of us walk past it in favour of more expensive and out-of-season produce. But listen up! It may well be considered food for the poor but nutritionally it is very rich. Cabbage contains phytochemicals that help fight cancer and reduce damage to our DNA. Cabbages are a great source of vitamin C – they have enough to prevent and cure scurvy. There's vitamin K that helps blood-clotting and protects against internal bleeding, b-carotene and other B-group vitamins, and calcium, potassium and fibre. Most of the goodness in cabbage is contained in the outer dark-green leaves, so it's important to buy fresh unsprayed cabbages, so that all the outer leaves can be eaten, too.

Raw cabbage juice is a proven remedy for peptic ulcers. If it doesn't sound appetising – and I'd be the first to complain if I had to take it – try mixing it with grape juice by juicing young cabbage leaves with a little water and slightly more than their weight of black grapes.

The humble cabbage is so full of goodness that it has kept nations alive in tough times – think kim chi, sauerkraut and the cabbage dishes of Ireland and soups of Europe. It has been increasingly overlooked in a world spoiled for choice because of the pong it gives off when it is overcooked. Poor cabbage – what an awkward legacy! However, dealing with the pong factor is easy and the easiest way to avoid it is down to how you cook it.

There is something to be said for introducing a little fat to cabbage. For

example, when stir-fried quickly in hot oil, the oil seals the cut surfaces of the cabbage and seems to stop the sulphur leaching out. Great! Cooked gently in olive oil or butter, just until it wilts and before the sulphur smell starts to waft out of the pot, it is deliciously sweet, slightly peppery and pleasantly crisp.

There are two ways to cook cabbage: slowly and quickly. When I grew up cabbage was only ever cooked slowly and, fortunately, in my home, it wasn't boiled to death. My mother served it with lashings of butter, and plenty of salt and make-you-sneeze ground white pepper. Doused with gravy and served alongside roasted meat it was fine fare. It also had a place nestling up to pan-fried sausages, fried onions and potato mash. And a weekend fry-up of bubble and squeak – mashed potatoes and cabbage – was pretty tasty. But I can't lie – it did smell, just a bit. Cabbage goes off the rails when it is kept in a warmer or bain-marie,

especially if it has been overcooked in the first place – it can't help but smell and taste bad.

Capers

Capers are the pickled or salted green flower buds of a shrub commonly found in the Mediterranean. The buds vary in size, and the smaller ones, which are the most difficult to harvest, fetch the highest prices. Non pareilles – small capers from France – are highly sought after as are those grown on the Italian island of Pantelleria. Larger capers are usually cheaper.

They develop capric acid during pickling and this, coupled with the added salt, gives the mineral salty tang most of us associate with capers. Capers packed in salt retain a better texture, maintaining a hint of the sea and a slight bitterness that's not as sharp as capers in brine. When buying capers in salt check that the salt is pure white; if it's tinged yellow or grey that indicates it's not fresh. Wash off loose salt then soak the capers in warm water for about 15 minutes. Drain and rinse again. If the capers still taste excessively salty, soak them again. Pat rinsed capers dry with paper towels before using. Stored in a cool dark pantry, salted capers will last for several months.

Capers packed in brine should be drained before use, then rinsed under running water and patted dry with paper towels. Once opened, capers in brine are best stored in the refrigerator, where they will last for many months. A white film on top of a jar of capers in brine is harmless; rinse it off.

Celery
Celery has a good amount of vitamin C, and calcium, potassium, sodium and fibre. Alternative and Oriental medicines make many health claims about celery – while many believe a phytochemical in celery helps lower blood pressure and cholesterol, this is yet to be proven.

Although celery is inherently a little bitter, spray residues on commercially grown celery make it even more so. The best advice is to wash the whole head of celery, lop off the top greenery and tips of stalks, then leave it to drain for 30 minutes before transferring it to a plastic bag and into the vegetable crisper. If you've got space in your refrigerator, stand the celery upright with the base of the stems in cold water and cover the top loosely with a plastic bag; this way it'll stay nice and crisp for more than a week. Every time you remove stalks they will need to be lightly scrubbed under running water before using them. It makes a significant difference to the taste of celery; I use a small soft brush that's kept for scrubbing vegetables.

Alternatively, search out organically grown celery from organic suppliers and farmers' markets.

If the celery is very stringy, run a vegetable peeler down the length of the celery sticks to quickly shave off the strings.

Cherries
Look for nice plump, smooth and shiny skinned blemish-free fruit, with green or supple stalks. Leave the stalks on the cherries if you're storing them as they help to keep them fresh. Eat any cherries with nicks or damaged skins soon after purchase and remove any soft or rotting cherries because one bad cherry can quickly affect others it is close to. Store cherries in the refrigerator – they deteriorate quickly at room temperature. Don't wash cherries until you are ready to use them as moisture causes them to decay.

Chicken fillet (tenderloin)
This is the long, thin pointy strip of tender meat that can easily be separated from the underside of the breast. Use sliced chicken breast as a substitute.

Chickpeas
Evidence suggests people have been eating chickpeas for 4000 years – that's an awfully long time. Legend tells us that the Roman orator Cicero had an ancestor with a wart on his face shaped like a chickpea and that is how they got their name *cecir* – now *ceci* in Italian. Whatever! Chickpeas are a relatively inexpensive but rich source of protein and iron, making them a useful addition to a vegetarian diet. The edible seeds of leguminous plants – also known as pulses – are usually twice as rich in protein as grains. This includes chickpeas and lentils. Chickpeas

specifically contain folate, vitamin E, potassium, copper and magnesium. Generally the only pulses that don't require soaking before cooking are lentils and split peas. Most other beans and peas are best soaked before cooking to allow them to fully rehydrate; it shortens the cooking time and makes them easier to digest. If you live in an area with hard water on tap, it is best to soak the pulses in boiled water; pulses absorb the calcium carbonate that makes water hard and that will increase the cooking time required, but the calcium carbonate is removed from water in steam when water is boiled. It is now known that using bicarbonate to soften water destroys vitamin B1 and so it is no longer recommended for cooking pulses and beans.

Some pulses, including chickpeas, can be toxic if not properly prepared. Discard the soaking water, boil them in fresh water for 10 minutes, drain, wipe out the pan, return them to the pan with fresh water and bring them back to the boil, then cook gently until tender. It might seem like a fiddle, but it ensures you've got rid of all the toxins.

Chillies
The popularity of chillies mystifies the experts, especially the bit about the pain they can inflict! Capsaicin, an alkaloid found mainly in the white membrane cushioning the seeds, is the bit that makes chillies hot. It's also an irritant that can burn skin and irritate cuts, causing varying degrees of pain. Wear disposable food gloves when handling chillies to prevent burning. However, some people believe when a bite of hot chilli burns the mouth the brain releases endorphins, which make you feel warm, relaxed, even high. What actually happens is this:

the capsaicin causes the blood vessels to dilate and increases circulation, then the body overheats and produces sweat. As the sweat evaporates it gives a cooling sensation on the skin – it's like your body's built-in air conditioning unit – that offers some relief, especially in hot countries. This helps explain their popularity in countries on and near the equator.

What about those hot-heads who chew their way through mounds of chillies at chilli-eating competitions? It seems they have fewer taste buds than the rest of us so it is easier for them to eat hot chillies without feeling pain. Water will not relieve a burning mouth, but there are two substances that will: dairy products and sugar. Yoghurt has an immediate cooling effect in the mouth and throat, and sugar in various forms helps neutralise capsaicin.

Chillies are also high up there as an antioxidant and contain plenty of vitamin C – more than tomatoes by weight. They also contain vitamin A. They seem to lower cholesterol and aid digestion. They are also used in homeopathic cures for rheumatism and arthritis.

It's not easy to judge how hot a chilli is just by looking at it, but the best guide is the size; generally, the smaller the chilli, the hotter it is, and the broader the chilli is at the shoulders, the milder it will be. Most recipes in this book call for hot chillies, and although you can lessen the buzz and use a milder chilli, or omit them from the recipe, many Asian dishes are a carefully balanced mix of hot, sour, sweet and salty. Without the punch of chilli they may well be too sweet, too salty or too sour.

Look for chillies that are firm and smooth, not soft and wrinkly. To store chillies, remove them from plastic packaging and wrap them loosely in paper towels. Put them in an uncovered container and keep them in the refrigerator for up to two weeks. See also Bird's eye chillies, on page 165.

Chorizo
Originating in Spain, chorizo sausage has many variations but always contains pork – usually fatty and coarsely ground – and smoked Spanish paprika that's called pimentón in Spain. Smoked paprika gives chorizo its distinctive red tinge and smoky flavour. Chorizo is often spiked with chilli and comes in varying degrees of hotness. It comes either as a fresh soft sausage that must be cooked, or in a dried form that is served sliced like salami. Mexican chorizo often contains beef as well as pork and the meat is more finely ground.

Coconut milk and coconut cream
Coconut milk and cream are extracted from the grated flesh of coconuts. Grated coconut is steeped in hot water, then pressed to extract the liquid known as coconut cream or thick coconut milk. A second steeping and pressing produces a thinner, less-creamy milk.

Canned coconut cream separates in the can into two distinct components: a rich cream and a watery liquid. Either scoop off the rich cream from the top and use as directed in curries, sauces or desserts and save the watery liquid to use in soups, curries or baking, or to cook coconut rice; or mix the contents of the can to form a smooth liquid. Store canned coconut cream in the refrigerator after opening but use it within two days.

Coriander roots

Coriander roots contain a lot of flavour and can be used in soups, curry pastes and curries. Wash them well and chop finely, or process to a paste in a liquidiser or food processor. They can be stored in a sealed plastic bag in the freezer until required.

Couscous, instant

The little dried semolina pellets that constitute instant couscous can be quickly softened in hot water or stock and served in place of rice or potatoes. Israeli couscous is a larger form.

Crème anglaise

This English-style pouring custard made with egg yolks, sugar and milk is often flavoured with vanilla. It is served, like cream, as an accompaniment to tarts, pies and fruit desserts or incorporated into sweet dishes such as ice-cream and trifle. It is available ready-made.

Creamy Dijonnaise mustard

This rich and creamy mustard flecked with crushed mustard seeds can be used more generously than smooth Dijon mustard; the flavour is quite mild. It's particularly good in dressings because it helps to thicken and emulsify the ingredients.

Cumin seeds, toasted

Toasting cumin seeds gives them a rich

earthy aroma and flavour. Put the seeds in a small, dry frying pan and set it over medium heat. Toast the seeds for a few minutes, shaking the pan occasionally until they start popping, darken in colour and smell fragrant. Grind the seeds in a spice grinder, or pulverise them with a mortar and pestle. Toast more than you need and store cooled seeds in an airtight jar.

Curry leaves

Curry leaves smell of, well, curry! These pointy-tipped leaves are richly scented and loaded with flavour. Use them fresh or dried for flavouring and garnish. Available from some Indian food stores, the plants are easy enough to grow and there is a bonus – they deter pests from the garden.

Eggs

As a precaution, it's advisable to avoid feeding eggs to children under 12 months old to prevent an egg allergy developing; although the egg yolks are not considered to be as much of a risk as the whites. It is best for the elderly, very young and others with weakened or compromised immune systems to avoid raw eggs.

Look for fresh eggs that have been kept chilled or stored in a cool environment and buy from places that have a fast turnover of stock. Transfer eggs to the refrigerator as soon after purchase as possible. While eggs in a wire basket or bowl may look cute in your kitchen, storing eggs at room temperature hastens their demise – 1 day in a warm kitchen is equal to 4 days in the refrigerator. Eggs have porous shells and should be stored in the cartons they come in, which offer some protection against other food aromas and bacteria. Keep them with the pointed end of the egg facing downwards to help slow moisture loss inside the egg. Fresh-laid eggs make the best poached eggs, and fresh eggs no more than 5 days old are usually best for cooking.

When it comes to hard-boiled eggs, eggs which are more than 5 days old are better because they're easier to peel. Despite the name hard-boiled – or hard-cooked in the US – eggs should never be cooked in furiously boiling water, nor over-cooked; it turns them rubbery and makes them unpalatable. Eggs cooked until the yolks are just setting, or are just set, are easier to eat and to digest than hard-boiled eggs. To cook perfect hard-boiled eggs for a salad, have eggs at room temperature and use the point of a dressmaking pin to prick the rounded end of the shell where there is a small air-filled sac. The air inside the egg can escape through this hole as the contents swell during cooking preventing the shell from cracking. (A cracked shell lets egg white escape in the water.) As soon as the eggs have finished cooking, pour off the water and let the cold tap run over them for several minutes until they feel cool. This cools them quickly and stops a grey ring from forming around the yolks.

When a recipe calls for a quantity of either egg whites or egg yolks, the unused egg whites or yolks can be stored for other uses. Egg whites will keep for several weeks in the refrigerator, or for several months if frozen. The trick is to remember how many egg whites are in the container!

If you forget, you can work it out by measuring the liquid:
2 egg whites = ¼ cup
4 egg whites = ½ cup.

Another trick is to calculate from the weight, knowing that the white makes up approximately two-thirds of an egg's weight and:
small or size 5 eggs weigh about 55g
medium or size 6 eggs weigh about 65g
large or size 7 eggs weigh about 75g.

Egg yolks will keep covered and refrigerated for up to three days. Spoon a little water over whole egg yolks to stop them forming a skin before covering them with plastic food wrap. Egg yolks can be frozen for up to a month but they will not be suitable for all types of cooking; they're only good for general jobs, such as acting as a binding agent for meatballs or for glazing pastry. Add a little salt to egg yolks before freezing.

All eggs used in the recipes in this book are free-range and organic.

Fennel

The herb fennel has many culinary uses. The feathery leaves can be used fresh as a herb and are particularly good with fish. The plant is also grown for its aromatic seeds which can be used in sweet and savoury dishes. Although native to the Mediterranean, fennel seed is a common spice in Indian cookery. The seeds are aromatic and warming with a mild spicy pungency. In India the seeds are eaten raw after a meal as a digestive. In Italy fennel seeds are often teamed with pork dishes, as pork takes longer to digest than most other meats. Fennel seed is also used in infant preparations for colic and can help adults suffering from flatulence. It's easy to grow your own fennel; buy the plants and let them run to seed. Harvest the seeds just before they ripen, while they're still supple and green. Air-dry them, then store airtight

– they're incredibly fragrant and, if you're not careful, everything in the pantry will smell of fennel!

Fennel bulbs

Florence fennel (*Foeniculum vulgare dulce*) forms a swollen stem underground. Referred to as a bulb, it is white, and crisp like celery, but with a distinctive aniseed flavour. Fresh and crisp, it can be eaten raw dunked into vinaigrette or sliced and used in salads; it has a real affinity with garlic, olive oil and parmesan cheese. It also makes an excellent cooked vegetable. It can be crumbed and fried, stewed, sauced, sautéed, roasted and barbecued. Cooking mutes its aniseedy flavour, making it taste more like celery.

Look for smooth white-skinned fennel bulbs without brown spots. The whole bulb is edible after trimming, but the outer pieces of mature fennel may be stringy and a bit tough; it's best to remove these. Wrap fennel tightly in plastic food wrap and keep refrigerated until ready to use. It'll keep fresh for 2–3 days, or about a week after picking.

If you've got a garden, try growing your own. The bulbs may not grow very large, but they'll be tender and sweet. Sow the seeds directly in the soil from mid-summer to early autumn – they're very easy to tend.

Feta

Traditionally, feta was made from sheep's or goat's milk, or a mixture of both. The milk was poured into pouches made from the stomach of a lamb or kid, or from leather, and stored in a warm atmosphere until the milk separated into curds and whey. The curds were compressed in baskets and the whey was salted and used as a brine to store the cheese.

The Greek or Bulgarian feta floating in milky, salty brine and sold in tins is as different from mass-produced feta as chalk is from cheese. Good traditional feta has a crumbly, flaky texture – it's not greasy, creamy or cloying. It has a slightly sour and mildly salty flavour and is virginal white – cow's milk feta has a yellowish tinge. It is at its best drizzled with olive oil and served with olives and tomatoes. In fact, a classic Greek salad has all these elements! The cheese is usually sliced, not crumbled, on top of a Greek salad – there may be some connection with the Italian word *fetta*, meaning slice.

Feta should not be unpleasantly salty. If it is too salty for your taste, soak it in cold water for 10 minutes, or up to two hours, to leach out the salt; it will taste much sweeter and milkier.

Feta works well in pies and cooked dishes because it holds its shape, and the saltiness works as a seasoning. It's delicious baked as it loses some salt and goes golden and fudgy. To bake feta, slice and place it on a baking sheet and grill or bake until golden. Crumble over salads.

Fish sauce

This thin, pungent sauce made from salted, fermented fish is the key flavouring in many Asian dishes. Not as revolting as it sounds, it works by seasoning the food rather than imparting a fishy flavour.

Garlic

Down the ages garlic has been used to prevent or cure almost every ailment known to man, including leprosy, plague, typhoid, dysentery, high blood-pressure, bronchitis, baldness, rheumatism, constipation and, even, a bad case of pimples!

The enduring claim that garlic contains antiseptic substances passed from folklore to fact last century. As recently as the First World War, the raw juice was used extensively on wounds to prevent them turning septic. And now, along with its antibacterial properties, garlic is acknowledged as an antiviral and anti-cancer agent. It is the sulphide in garlic that makes it antiseptic. Other health benefits are substantial, too. Garlic is most effective dealing to stomach bacteria, and research continues into garlic's role in preventing stomach ulcers and stomach and colon cancers.

Garlic is delicious when young and fresh, when it is as crisp and juicy as a just-picked apple. But store it we must, or we'll have none to last us through the year. It keeps better if strung up in a plait in a cool, airy place. Most of us buy garlic in corms – known as bulbs – and the best place to store these is in the vegetable crisper in the refrigerator. Take off only the cloves you need, because the cloves will stay moister if attached to the base.

How many times have you heard someone say, 'Garlic repeats on me'? Contrary to what many people believe, garlic aids digestion. The green sprout in the centre of older cloves is the culprit. Once it starts to sprout it loses the sweet taste and juicy flesh of young garlic. Thankfully, it is easy to cut each clove in half and pick out the sprout with the point of a sharp knife. Shrivelled and yellowing garlic should be thrown out – it can ruin a dish, especially if used raw.

Garlic can be quite sharp tasting; it can also increase the heat of a dish with its pungency. When garlic is crushed, a chemical reaction takes place as the cells are broken down; crushed paste and garlic juice are very potent. If you want less of a hot bite from garlic, chop it, or if you prefer a milder flavour still, slice it. Garlic is strongest used raw, and mellows during cooking – the longer you cook it, the milder it becomes. Garlic with smaller corms and purplish skin tend to be the hottest.

Ginger
When ginger is very young and fresh, it's crisp and doesn't need peeling; at this stage it has a mild flavour and can be used liberally. It adds a hot fresh bite to food and when mixed with other spices and chillies, increases the hotness of a dish. Look for plump, firm clumps of ginger – called hands – and avoid any that are withered as they will be pungent with coarse fibres. The best way to store it and prevent it from rotting is to wrap it in paper towels and keep it in the vegetable crisper. Discard it when it begins to shrivel. It can also be kept in the freezer in a resealable plastic bag, but frozen ginger is best cooked.

Hazelnuts
Unless hazelnuts are very fresh, they are best toasted to develop a rich roasted-nut taste with a mild coffee-like flavour. The skins are easily removed after toasting, making the nuts less bitter to eat. To toast hazelnuts, put them in a shallow ovenproof dish and toast in an oven preheated to 180°C for 10–12 minutes, or until you can see the nuts have coloured through the burst skins. Tip nuts onto an old clean cloth, bundle up and rub vigorously to remove skins. Store airtight.

For nutritional information see Nuts, on p. 176.

Herbs
Got to www.juliebiuso.com for information about herbs.

Kaffir lime leaves
The makrut lime tree is grown mainly for its unusual-looking, double-pointed, strongly scented leaves. The trees bear fragrant warty-looking fruit that, despite not containing much juice, can be zested like regular limes. Excess lime leaves can be frozen in a sealed plastic bag but they're only good for cooking as they tend to discolour and go limp once they are thawed. Fresh leaves can be stored in a sealed plastic bag in the refrigerator for 2–3 weeks.

The fresh leaves smell somewhat sweeter than lime zest, fresh and citrusy clean. With the centre ribs removed, they can be rolled and sliced exceedingly thin for adding to uncooked dishes. Whole leaves can be added to curries, stuffed inside fish or floated in soups.

There's no real substitute other than the lime. If fresh leaves aren't available, use lime or lemon zest instead. Don't be tempted to use dried leaves because they lack intensity and are often musty.

Kecap manis
Also known as ketjap manis, this Indonesian thick and sweet soy sauce – made from soya beans, palm sugar and spices, including star anise – is available from Asian food stores. Refrigerate after opening.

Lamb backstrap
This boneless lean piece of meat is about 20 centimetres long and weighs around 200 grams. It is cut from the middle loin and is obtained by removing the rack and cutting between the twelfth and thirteenth ribs. It is also

known as lamb shortloin.

Lamb tenderloins
Like an eye fillet of beef, this is the most-tender cut of lamb. It is a small lean strip, 2–3 centimetres thick and, once trimmed, it is about 20 centimetres; the grain runs lengthways. You will need to remove the silverskin before cooking. Allow two per person, and cook very briefly; 2–3 minutes all up.

Lemon grass
Lemon grass is a tall perennial grass used extensively for flavouring throughout South-east Asia. The green leaves of the plant can be used for infusions, but it is their squat base which is called for in cooking. The tough outer leaves at the base of the stems are peeled away to reveal a soft, pale centre. Lemon grass stems are either smashed with a mallet and added whole to infuse soups and curries with their scent, or pounded to a paste, or sliced. It's important to slice stems crossways – long fibres will be detectable in a finished dish. If fresh lemon grass stems are not available, use lemon peel instead.

Lemons
If you have a lemon tree in your garden you have a friend in the garden! Just be kind to it. To remove a lemon from the tree, twist the lemon until it pops free – don't pull it. If you pull it, a lump of peel can remain on the stalk left on the tree and this may rot and prevent lemons from growing in the future.

There is a lot of confusion between lemons. For the record, meyer lemons, with their often bumpy-skinned, large, round, fleshy fruit that have sweetish juice and pith, are not true lemons. They're a hybrid; probably a cross between a lemon and an orange or mandarin – the thin, deep-yellow skin is often tinged with shades of orange.

Cooks love them because they're easy to squeeze and yield plenty of juice, and gardeners love them, too, because they bear fruit for most of the year. However, they are sweeter than a true lemon, and sometimes do not add enough acidity to a dish. Meyer lemons are more exuberant than Lisbon lemons and are better suited to cutting the oiliness of a gin and tonic, in my opinion, but they are often too sweet for Asian and Mediterranean dishes that require the bracing freshness of a Lisbon lemon.

More often than not it's a case of using what I've got, but if I could choose I'd use meyer lemons to squeeze over barbecued or grilled fish and cutlets, or to rub over a chicken before roasting; and I'd use Lisbon lemons for Asian and Mediterranean dishes, vinaigrettes, lemon tarts, and in dishes calling for a more-concentrated lemon flavour.

Lemons are easier to squeeze when they're at room temperature, but they can rot in humid conditions. Keep one or two in the fruit bowl, and the rest refrigerated, or leave them on the tree until you need them. If lemons are very cold, or are not very juicy, roll them several times with your hand to help release the juice, or warm them in a microwave before squeezing. An average lemon will yield around 1 tablespoon of grated zest and 2½ tablespoons of juice.

If you're lucky enough to have a glut of lemons, squeeze and strain the juice and pour it into ice-cube trays to freeze. Once frozen, pack the cubes into plastic bags. Thaw as required.

Lemon-infused olive oil
Extra virgin oil, either olive or avocado, infused with citrus essences adds an intense flavour to food. If not available, use extra virgin oil to which a little finely grated zest and juice of a lemon has been added. Oils infused with lime and mandarin are also available.

Limoncello
Sometimes spelled lemoncello, this lemon liqueur of Italian origin must be served icy cold to numb its sweetness. Perhaps at its best poured over perfectly ripe sliced strawberries, it's also good mixed with lightly whipped cream in a sponge sandwich or drizzled over vanilla ice cream and berries. Keep it in the refrigerator and pop it in the freezer 30 minutes before serving.

Mangoes
The flesh of this aromatic fruit is an excellent source of vitamin A. The fleshy parts on either side of the large flattish fibrous stone in the centre are called the cheeks. It's usually best to peel a mango and that is easily done with a potato peeler. The cheeks can then be cut off as close to the stone as possible, then any additional flesh.

The stone is the cook's perk – there's nothing better than standing at the sink, mango juice dribbling down your chin, prising off the last of the sweet flesh with your teeth even if you'll need to have a good floss afterwards!

Mascarpone
Mascarpone is sometimes described as a cheese but it is actually a thick, rich cream with a high fat content – around 48 per cent. It is usually made from cow's milk by adding a culture to the cream, then heating the cream and leaving it to thicken; a good mascarpone is thick enough to support

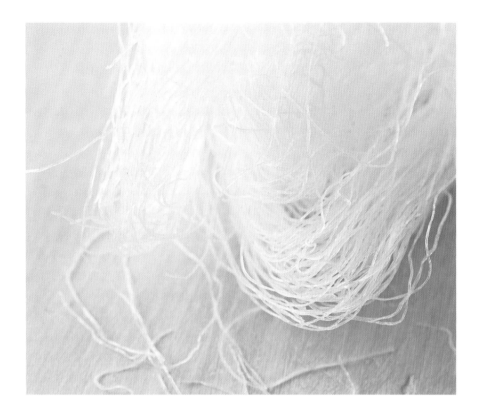

a spoon. It's used in sweet dishes, such as tiramisu, and savoury dishes, for example pasta sauces. It helps thicken mixtures and adds richness, smoothness and a velvety texture.

Minced meat

The most important point with minced meat is to use it as fresh as possible. The extra handling and exposure to the air make it more vulnerable than chunks of meat – a joint of meat will keep fresher longer than sliced or cubed meat, which will keep fresh longer than minced meat. Try to buy minced meat the day you intend to cook it, or, at the most, the day before. Also known as ground meat or simply as mince, it is often sold off at a special price in supermarkets to which I say, 'Caveat emptor! Let the buyer beware!' Any meat marked 'special clearance' or 'reduced' is not being sold with the shelf-life of fresh meat – always check the packing date, not the use-by date.

Mincing your own meat is a good way to control what cuts of meat and the amount of fat you eat. Just keep in mind that, although fat-free this and fat-free that may be the order of the day, when it comes to minced beef – and to a lesser degree minced lamb – you need a certain amount of fat to keep it moist and to provide succulence. If you want burgers, meatballs and meat sauce with the texture of sawdust then, by all means, use 99% fat-free mince!

Mozzarella, bocconcini

Mozzarella was traditionally made from buffalo's milk, but it is more usual these days to find cow's milk mozzarella. *Mozzarella di bufala* has a high moisture content and a delicate, sweet, milky-earthy flavour. It is softer, creamier and melts more easily than cow's milk mozzarella. It should be sold swimming in whey.

Bocconcini is the Italian name for small bite-sized balls of mozzarella. When lightly smoked it is known as *mozzarella affumicata*, and when heavily smoked it is sold as *scamorza*.

Mozzarella, whether it is made from cow's or buffalo's milk, doesn't have a huge flavour on its own, but it absorbs flavour well. It provides body and texture to dishes and, of course, it melts and goes all gooey.

Muscovado
A raw sugar with a strong taste of molasses that adds plenty of flavour to rich fruit cakes, boiled fruit cakes and other dried fruit baking, and is good in chutneys and pickles where a dark colour is welcome (if you want light-coloured pickles, use white sugar). Pass it through a coarse sieve before using.

Mushrooms
It's usually not necessary to wash mushrooms before use; if mushroom cups fill with water during washing it oozes out during cooking and makes the mushrooms watery. Just wipe them with a damp cloth. You won't even need to peel cultivated mushrooms. Mushrooms contain a lot of moisture of their own and, if you cook them slowly, the liquid will come out. This is fine when you want them to be part of a stew or in a soup but not so good when you want mushrooms on not-soggy toast.

For mushrooms to go on toast and in omelettes, tartlets and the like, choose small, tightly closed mushrooms, slice them thickly and cook them over high heat for a short period. Get the pan nice and hot, then put a decent knob of butter in the pan and as it is sizzling, almost on the point of frothing and browning, tip in the mushrooms; don't

crowd the pan or they'll stew. Toss them once or twice – no more – or the juices will run out. Seared so the moisture stays inside, you'll bite into juicy mushrooms, bursting with flavour, with gorgeous crisp browned edges and a hint of browned nutty butter. Scrumptious!

If you have a choice, pack loose mushrooms in a brown paper bag when buying them – it keeps the mushrooms drier. Mushrooms don't like to get sweaty and will rot quickly if kept in a damp bag. Many mushrooms are sold packed on trays lined with an absorbent pad, and these store the mushrooms well for about a week. If there is no absorbent pad or you have bought loose mushrooms, transfer the mushrooms to a container lined with paper towels and store them in the refrigerator until required.

Noodles
Cellophane noodles are round, slightly transparent, noodles generally made from mung bean starch, or some other vegetable starch. Very thin ones are called vermicelli, and they are also known as bean thread noodles and glass noodles. They are great in salads.

Rice noodles come in a variety of thicknesses and go under various names. 'Rice stick noodles' refer to dried rice noodles which are generally flat, though they can be thick or thin. Vermicelli noodles made from rice are whiter than cellophane noodles and are not translucent.

Nuts
All nuts are nutritious, containing a range of minerals and vitamins, and a good amount of protein, making them particularly useful in a vegetarian diet. If walnuts or almonds are eaten

in combination with a whole grain their protein content is equal to that of meat! Most nuts contain vitamin E, a powerful antioxidant. Most are also high in fat, but fortunately it's mostly unsaturated fat – that's the healthy kind that lowers harmful cholesterol.

It's important to eat nuts fresh; old or rancid nuts will mar the flavour of any dish they are added to and they are difficult to digest. They may even cause stomach upsets and affect digestion. Eaten regularly, they can have a harmful toxic affect. It's easy to detect the 'off' smell of rancid nuts – they smell like butter which has been left for too long at room temperature. Most fresh nuts are creamy-coloured and rancid nuts usually show signs of yellowing. Discard nuts that are showing signs of mould, traces of dirt or insect infestation.

Nuts in the shell will keep fresh for up to a year. Whole nuts with their skins on will keep fresher for longer than blanched, sliced, slivered, chopped or ground nuts.

Walnuts can be toasted or sizzled gently in a little butter or oil. After toasting, rub them gently and try and remove as much of the skin as possible because it is bitter-tasting.

Keep nuts in an airtight container away from light in the pantry or in the refrigerator. For longer storage, you can keep them in the freezer. Use frozen nuts straight from the freezer; they do not need thawing. While organically grown nuts may be a little more expensive, they are generally fresher and worth paying a premium for.

Olive oil
Olive oil is sensitive to light and warmth. Exposure to light soon turns

the oil rancid, giving it an unpleasant buttery taste, so be aware that bottles of oil may look pretty on a kitchen bench, but if the oil is for consumption it should be kept in the pantry. Dark glass offers more protection than clear glass; avoid oil in plastic bottles. Don't refrigerate olive oil because any condensation which forms on the inside of the bottle top will fall back into the oil.

Olives
I recommend using well-drained firm black olives for the recipes in this book unless otherwise stated. If olives are exceptionally salty, soak them in a bowl of cold water – even 30 minutes will help. Either remove the pits with an olive pitter or warn your guests that the dish contains whole olives to avoid anyone accidentally chomping on an olive stone. Avoid buying pitted black olives; they lose much of their flavour during processing. Large green Queen olives with their meaty texture and sweet and mildly briny flavour are good for using in cooked dishes and on kebabs because they hold together well.

Oregano, Greek or Sicilian
Particularly aromatic varieties of dried oregano. Available from specialty food stores. If not available, use fresh marjoram, or dried oregano.

Orzo
Orzo is one of several small pastina – little pasta shapes – specifically designed to be served in light soups, or to amuse small children. Orzo takes its name from barley and is shaped like barley seeds. Other popular shapes include peppercorns, melon seeds, alphabet letters, rings and rice grains called risoni. Risoni is similar in shape to orzo and can be used in the same way.

Palm sugar
Palm sugar is made from the sap extracted from young palms, boiled down to a thick syrup and dehydrated into discs. It has an intense, sweet

caramel-like flavour. Grate or chop before use. Store any leftover grated palm sugar in an airtight container.

Panko crumbs

These dry Japanese crumbs have a coarse texture, crumble easily and store very well providing they are kept in an airtight container. Panko crumbs are particularly crisp and crunchy and can be used on their own or mixed with parmesan and butter as a topping, or used to coat food for frying. They can also be used in stuffings in place of fresh breadcrumbs; in that case it may pay to use slightly less or add a bit more liquid as they are drier than fresh breadcrumbs.

Paprika

Paprika is generally made from *Capsicum annum*, otherwise known as pepper or capsicum. Paprika is believed to have originated in Hungary after peppers arrived from the New World. Hungarian paprika is a striking bright red with a mild sweet flavour, although hotter grades are available. Smoked Spanish paprika is not so brightly coloured; it's more of a dusty red with a strong capsicum aroma and smoky notes that give it a more complex flavour than chilli powder. It comes in sweet, bittersweet and hot strengths. Like cayenne, paprika is high in vitamin C and other nutrients, and many of the health benefits accredited to cayenne also apply to paprika.

Parmesan

Parmesan (Parmigiano Reggiano) is the most famous Italian hard cheese. In Italy it is called grana because of its granular structure. It's quite probable that grana cheese was being made as far back as 800BC. Parmesan itself evolved from an old Etruscan recipe sometime during the 10th and 11th

centuries and became increasingly popular from the 13th century onwards, as various poetic and culinary documents illustrate.

The making and maturing of Parmesan is a strictly controlled affair, centred around the city and province of Parma – from which the cheese took its name centuries ago – and the provinces of Reggio Emilia and Modena. Parmesan is made in exactly the same way today as it was by artisan cheese makers in the 14th century. It is a non-processed cheese, made from fresh unpasteurised milk. Cheese-makers, who are supplied twice a day with cow's milk straight after milking, make batches of cheese every day. This means that the cheese factories must be situated close to the farms and it's for this reason that it is – and always will be – a small-scale operation.

Parmesan has an intoxicating aroma and a spicy flavour with fruity overtones and an interesting granular texture. It is one of the glories of this world. Just think – there are not many recipes which have remained unchanged for seven centuries. Parmesan look-alikes tend to be highly seasoned, soapy, dry, coarse-textured or inferior in some way. Authentic parmesan melts without running, browns well, isn't greasy and doesn't become rubbery. It is quickly digested – even by infants – and low in calories.

Buy it in one piece, wrap it in waxed paper then aluminum foil and store it in the door or the coolest part of the refrigerator. Replace the waxed paper every time you rewrap it and wipe the rind if it shows sign of moisture. It will store well for a month or two, but will eventually become dry and strong. Grate parmesan as required,

because it quickly loses its aroma and flavour. Parmesan can be frozen treble-wrapped in aluminium foil for up to 6 months, but it will be crumblier and slightly drier when thawed and should be used within a week.

Pesto

Pesto, which means 'pounded', usually refers to the rich, green, oily sauce made with basil, garlic, pine nuts, olive oil and parmesan and Romano cheeses. In Italy they say the best basil is a small-leafed plant that grows in Liguria, close to the sea. If you live on the coast, plant basil in full sun, facing the ocean, and see if you can detect a stronger, sweeter fragrance. Now other pestos made with walnuts, capers, olives etc. are also popular.

Pomegranate syrup/molasses

Pomegranate syrup is made by cooking down the juicy seeds of fresh pomegranates until syrupy. The syrup can be reduced further until sticky and thick to form pomegranate molasses. The flavour is more sour than sweet. It is used as a souring agent, like tamarind or balsamic vinegar, to give a complex sweet and sour flavour. Store in the refrigerator after opening and use within six months.

Potatoes

Potatoes are described as waxy, all-purpose or floury.

Waxy or new potatoes are waxy because their sugar has not yet converted to starch, as it will with age. Waxy potatoes are good for salads because the potato holds together after slicing or dicing. And if you want to add potatoes to a casserole, use waxy ones because, again, they will hold their shape. They're also the potatoes to slice for a gratin as floury potatoes

will turn to fluff. Most freshly dug spring potatoes, such as jersey bennes, early season desiree, early season Duke of York, draga, concorde, maris anchor, nicola and kipfler will all fit the bill.

A floury potato is low in moisture and sugar and high in starch. Floury potatoes are excellent for mashing and for roasting and cooking in embers. They also make good French fries and wedges. Floury potatoes are the right ones to use to thicken soups because they will dissolve into the soup thickening the liquid. Agria, rua, Dakota, russet Burbank, Sebago and King Edward are good examples.

All-purpose potatoes do most jobs reasonably well, but may not shine in any one. To complicate the issue, some potatoes start off waxy at the beginning of their season, but become less so as the season progresses. For instance, new-season desiree are good steamed and dressed with a vinaigrette,

and it's later in the season that they will make a good purée. Ilam Hardy potatoes, too, start off waxy, and become starchy later in the season.

Prawns

Most of the prawns we buy are frozen; they've been snap-frozen at sea or just after catching, or kept in an ice-slurry until the fishing boat reaches shore, then frozen. Frozen prawns will keep for several months in the freezer before they start to lose condition. Some recipe books advise to thaw frozen prawns slowly in the fridge, but prawn experts will tell you otherwise – thaw them quickly to preserve moisture, flavour and texture. This is easily done by putting the prawns in a sealed plastic bag if they are not already in

one and immersing the bag in a sink of hot water; the water should not be boiling, just hand-hot. As the water cools, change it, until the prawns are no longer stiff. They do not have to be completely thawed in the water as they will continue thawing as you rinse and pat them dry and start to prepare the dish. Some recipes suggest thawing the prawns in warm water without the protection of a bag, but they will lose flavour.

There are two main points to make here: prawns are quick to defrost so there's no point buying defrosted prawns that may have been hanging around defrosted for a day or two – you can't tell just by looking when they were thawed. Remember, too, that seafood quickly loses condition at room temperature. The equation is one hour at warm room temperature is equal to 24 hours of refrigerated life.

Prawns are sold either raw or cooked. Again, you don't know how they were cooked and you can't tell when they were cooked just by looking at them. It's safest to cook them yourself. And, if you are intending to use the prawns in a hot dish, always buy raw prawns or the prawns end up being cooked twice, which can make them dry or rubbery.

Prawns have a digestive tract running the length of their bodies and this is sometimes visible as a black or orangey vein. It won't make you ill if you eat it, but it is gritty to the bite and can be off-putting. If it is visible, it needs to be removed. Run the tip of a small sharp knife down the back of the prawn and gently pull out the vein, then rinse the prawn. It is sometimes possible to pull the vein out from the tail end of the prawn without slitting the back; this is easier to do if the shell has been removed. Some prawns have had the digestive tract removed when you buy them.

Prosciutto
Sometimes referred to as Parma ham, prosciutto is sold in two forms: raw and cooked. *Prosciutto crudo* is a raw ham cured by air and salt and not, as is often presumed, by smoking. It is sweet and delicate with creamy, sweet-tasting fat. It is sliced very thin with a strip of the sweet-tasting fat attached to every slice; the fat is part of the experience, giving the cured meat a softer edge. It can be served as an antipasto component, used to wrap around food, or added to stuffings and pasta sauces. *Prosciutto cotto* is cooked ham. In this book, prosciutto always refers to the raw, cured ham.

Quark
A soft, creamy white fresh curd cheese made from whole, skimmed or semi-skimmed milk. Thicker than Greek yoghurt, with a mild lemony tang, it's smooth texture makes it a perfect choice for dips and cheesecakes.

Quinoa
Quinoa is a small nutritious seed which has been cultivated in the Andes since at least 3000BC. It has been tagged a 'superfood' because of its high protein, calcium and iron content; it also has several B-group vitamins and many other valuable nutrients. The seeds are coated in a bitter-tasting substance called saponin, and although most of this is washed off after harvesting, my advice is to put it in a sieve and give it a thorough rinse under running water before cooking; this applies especially to organically grown quinoa. Cook it in gently boiling water until tender – between 12 and 18 minutes although organically-grown quinoa may take a bit longer. Tip it into a fine sieve, and if not serving hot, make some steam holes through it with the end of a skewer and leave it to drain before mixing with a dressing of your choice. Quinoa has a wheaty, nutty flavour, and it's good hot, tossed with a knob of butter and a clove of crushed garlic, or a sprinkling of herbs or spices. It's also good cold in salads and in stuffed vegetables.

Raspberries
Raspberries are generally red in colour, although there are deep-red and black fruits, and paler coloured raspberries, too. They contain more fibre than most other fruits and one cup of raspberries will provide half your daily Vitamin C requirement. And then there's folic acid, manganese, copper and iron. In all, raspberries are an excellent source of antioxidants, especially red and black raspberries because they are full of anthocyanins – the blue, red and violet pigment found in plants.

Raspberries are fragile, however, and they need cosseting. Unlike blackberries, which retain their central white core when they are picked, raspberries are hollow and can easily be squashed. Washing makes them go soft and it will dilute their flavour; also, if raspberries are stored after washing they will quickly rot. If you must wash them, do so with a minimal amount of water and pat them dry with paper towels just before they are required. Never soak raspberries or they'll turn into waterlogged blobs.

Raspberries are infinitely more flavoursome at room temperature than chilled, so remember to bring them out of the refrigerator 30 minutes before serving.

To keep raspberries and blackberries in pristine condition, transfer them to shallow plastic containers lined with paper towels, cover with more paper towels and keep them in the refrigerator.

Refreshing
This means to rinse with water. Vegetables are refreshed with a cup or two of cold water after blanching or cooking for any of the following reasons: to halt the cooking process; to remove strong flavours; and to help keep the colour. To refresh pasta or rice, use warm water; cold water makes starchy ingredients turn tacky.

Ricotta
Although classified as a cheese, ricotta is really a milk product being a by-

product of the cheese making process. It is made from whey after it has been separated from the curd. The whey is heated and the ricotta forms on the surface – the curds and whey have already been heated so this second heating gives its name to the product; ricotta means re-cooked.

Ricotta has a delicate milky flavour and should be soft in texture, unlike other curd or cottage cheeses, making it easy to blend with other ingredients. It can be eaten as it is, sweetened with sugar and eaten with fruit, or used in sweet dishes, pies, cakes and tortes and in savoury fillings for pasta dishes and meats.

Saffron

The world's most expensive spice, the orange-gold threads of saffron are the stigmas of *Crocus sativus*. They are hand-harvested one by one and dried in the sun or artificially. In Spain the stigmas are toasted over charcoal. The best saffron is rich in colour and highly aromatic, musky, pungent and slightly bitter, but it loses its zest on keeping. Store it away from light and in an airtight jar. Saffron is often lightly toasted in a dry frying pan to develop flavour before use.

Salad greens

All salad greens should be washed before use, even if organically grown. Although my late Italian mother-in-law, Mamma Rosa, had a neat habit of bundling the greens in an oversized clean tea towel and spinning the bundle gently so the water was squeezed out, I recommend a salad spinner for drying the greens. It's easy to be too vigorous and end up bruising the delicate leaves.

Salt

Salt is the most indispensable ingredient in the kitchen. It draws out nuances of flavour that, had the food been left unsalted, may have lain dormant. Compensating for not using salt in the cooking by sprinkling it on the cooked food is not the same – you are likely to taste only salt. Sea salt comprises small crystalline flakes of salt. A good one is completely natural, has no additives or bitter aftertaste and has a less aggressive taste than common table salt. Sea salt flakes are easily crumbled and dissolved in dressings and sauces. Rock salt is much harder and should not be used in dressings as it takes too long to dissolve, nor is it recommended for sprinkling on top of baked items, such as Italian breads, because it becomes hard during baking – hard enough to crack teeth. However, it's the cheapest salt so I use it for salting water to cook pasta and vegetables.

Sambal oelek

Sometimes spelled sambal ulek and sambal olek, it is available as a prepared condiment. Made from pounded chillies, salt and vinegar or tamarind, a sambal – meaning relish or sauce – is used to spice up dishes.

Sesame oil

Pressed from toasted sesame seeds, sesame oil is very nutritious. It's not really used for cooking – it is too strong, too thick and too expensive. It is used more as a condiment, added at the end of cooking or drizzled over food before serving.

Shallots

Shallots are a species of onion that form clusters of small bulbs. They're generally milder and slightly sweeter than onions and less pungent

than garlic, although they possess characteristics of both. They are particularly high in anti-cancer compounds, help lower cholesterol and blood-pressure, and help 'thin' blood and prevent clotting. Their natural antibiotics help with bronchitis, colds and flu. They're a good source of vitamins B6, C and A, and folate, and are more easily digested than regular brown onions, especially when cooked.

Look for shallots that feel heavy and firm – not papery and dry – and that are not sprouting or showing any signs of mould or insect infestation. Store them in a cool dry place, in a ventilated bag or basket. They will sprout and go soft if stored in a warm place and if stored in plastic, they will soon rot. Storing shallots in the refrigerator is not recommended because it encourages mould but, like onions, chilling shallots for several hours or overnight before peeling will bring about fewer tears when chopping them.

Shallots can be eaten raw, enhancing dressings and sauces, or chopped first, halved or left whole and cooked. They are also good sliced and caramelised and they are often used in many Asian dishes as a garnish. They can also be pickled in the same manner as pickled onions, but they will be milder in flavour.

How much is one shallot? It's confusing, because most shallot 'bulbs' will break apart into two or more bulbs when peeled. If a recipe calls for one shallot, use the entire bulb, but you'll have to make a decision about whether to choose a large or a small shallot – they vary enormously. Recipes often call for chopped shallot, which is easier to measure accurately. Small shallots tend to be milder than large ones, but

large ones are easier to peel.

A good rule of thumb is to choose a small shallot for a delicate dish, or when the shallot is used raw, and a larger shallot for a more robust, cooked dish.

Shallots, crisp fried

You can cook sliced shallots gently for 30–40 minutes until crisp or buy them ready-made from Asian food stores. Sprinkle them over dishes or add to peanut sauces or condiments. They're wonderfully sweet and mildly pungent.

Sherry vinegar

Sherry vinegar, or more correctly *vinagre de Jerez* (or *Xeres*), is made in oak barrels previously used for ageing sherry. It's made on the same solera system as sherry, in a network of barrels. It's golden brown and clear, not syrupy like balsamic, but it can be just as beguiling, just as addictive . . . It has a bracing spicy sharpness that is warming in the chest like an aged red wine; there are nuances of roasted nuts, caramel, oak and sweet floral spices. You could say a good aged sherry vinegar possesses all the complexity of a fine wine, and is just as revered as *balsamic tradizionale*. A salad with robust ingredients will show it off but it adds a sparkle, a fresh note and a welcome tang to soups, stuffings, gravies, sauces and stews, and seafood and vegetable tapas. Use it, also, to deglaze pans or in marinades as a tenderiser.

Smoked fish

Curing food with smoke is an ancient process developed to preserve food but these days, thanks to refrigeration, it's more about enhancing the flavour of food and creating a tasty convenience food. Smoked fish is ready to eat as it is, with nothing more than a squirt of lemon juice and twist of the peppermill. It can be flaked into salads and used in sandwiches and dips, too. It doesn't need any extra cooking, but it can be cooked, and is good added to soups,

pies and tarts, and leftovers can be used up in omelettes or rice dishes, such as kedgeree.

A smoked fish will keep in the refrigerator for about five days, but the best smoked fish is fresh from the smoker, when it's moist and succulent. Plan to use smoked fish as soon after smoking, or purchase, as you can. When I want smoked fish, I ring around my local fishmongers and find who has fish just coming out of the smoker – that way I know what I buy is going to be deliciously moist. Small fish dry out more during smoking, so choose bigger fish.

Smoked fish will store quite well wrapped first in greaseproof paper then newspaper. Put the fish in a plastic bag and keep it refrigerated. Bring the fish to room temperature before taking it off the bone because it will come away from the bones and skin more readily when at room temperature. (However, this doesn't apply to hot-smoked salmon which is oily and easily skinned and flaked at any temperature). Hot-smoked fish has less of a smoky flavour than cold-smoked fish and it's a matter of preference.

Strawberries
Strawberries are at their sweetest and best when picked fully ripe. Berries picked before then don't go on to develop the gorgeous sweetness that taste of summer. If you want to keep strawberries in pristine condition, line a shallow plastic container with paper towels and put in a layer of strawberries – two layers at most – discarding any imperfect ones as you go. Cover with another piece of paper and keep refrigerated but away from icy areas in the refrigerator. Remember to bring the strawberries to room temperature

before serving because chilling mutes their fragrance and flavour.

Do strawberries need to be washed before eating? Common sense tells us they should, because they grow close to the earth, and are handled by pickers and packers. But water dilutes the sweet juice, making strawberries flavourless, and it softens their texture, making them spongy. Their intoxicating sweet fragrance washes off, like perfume. Keeping the stems intact until you've washed strawberries can help, and shaking them thoroughly, then patting them dry with paper towels can help a little, too. But, the best strawberry is one plucked fully ripe from the plant at the end of a long, dry day. You probably know to never go strawberry picking after a downpour but, when it comes to washing them, well, if no one's watching . . .

Sumac
A coarse powder made from the ripe, reddish-brown berries of the sumac shrub, sumac brings a refreshing note to many Middle Eastern dishes. The lemony taste and mild astringency works well with roasted or grilled chicken, meat or fish. It's also good sprinkled over tomatoes drizzled with a little oil before baking, or stirred into yoghurt to accompany meat dishes. Store airtight.

Sweet corn
The best corn is fresh corn, corn grown near you, corn that hasn't had to travel miles, and corn that is cooked and devoured as soon as possible after picking. Fresh corn is a high-carbohydrate food, with good quantities of vitamins A and B, and some C. It contains potassium, moderate amounts of protein and hardly any fat.

For those lucky few who are able to grow their own sweet corn, putting the water on to boil just before picking the corn is sage advice. Here's the rub: as soon as corn is cut from the plant, its sugar starts turning to starch, so the sooner you get it in the pot, the sweeter it's going to be. New varieties of corn retain the sugar for a little longer but the same rule applies – the sooner it's cooked after picking, the better.

Buy corn on the day you intend to cook it, and be fussy in the selection. A large pile of corn stacked high generally indicates a delivery of fresh corn. If you're scrabbling around over the last half dozen cobs trying to pick the best, you're probably better to take corn off the menu until the next delivery arrives. Ask when that's likely to be, and plan your menu accordingly. A good display of corn might be topped with one husked cob to show the quality, but avoid buying corn that has been stripped of its husk and silk because these keep the corn moist.

While most of us enjoy eating corn on the cob, some people prefer it off the cob. That's easily done; simply slice the hot kernels off the cob with a sharp knife. Eat the kernels hot with dobs of melting butter and loads of salt and pepper or stuff them into generously buttered bread rolls – the warmth of the kernels melts the butter. Yum!

Of course, there's plenty more that can be done with cobs of corn but, for my money, the best way to eat corn on the cob is in private. Party food it is not, nor is it the thing to serve to a hot date. Simply select your corn, cook it briefly, drain it and, as soon as it has cooled enough to handle, slather it with butter and season it with plenty

of salt and pepper if you like it. Then sit in a corner where no one can see you, or bend over the kitchen sink and stuff your face with it. Away from prying eyes you don't have to worry about butter dribbling down your chin and corn getting stuck between your teeth. That's how corn should be eaten!

Choose corn with supple green husks. If the husks are dry and yellowing and the silks brown and dry, the corn is past its best. Once the husk is removed, the silk should feel silky and slippery, and almost moist. The kernels should threaten to squeak when you touch them and they should feel slightly moist. The kernels should be plump and when pressed they should exude milky liquid.

To cook the cobs in their husks, remove the silks first. Pull down the husks leaf by leaf, remove the silks, then rewrap the cob carefully with the husks; tie with string if necessary. Soak the corn cobs in cold water for 15–30 minutes. Cook over hot coals for 15–30 minutes, turning often. The corn will steam and become tender. The moisture prevents burning but, once the water has evaporated, the sugars will caramelise and develop a rich, sweet flavour. Alternatively, cook the corn cobs on a barbecue hot plate, basting with a little water from time to time.

If you're worried about butter, try fresh barbecued corn drizzled with a fruity, estate-bottled extra virgin olive oil.

Tahini
This thick, oily paste made from toasted sesame seeds is also known as tahina. Mix with yogurt and garlic or with cooked, mashed eggplant and garlic to make a delicious dip.

Tamarind pulp
Tamarind pulp is obtained from the pods of the tamarind tree. Tamarind is a good source of vitamin B and calcium. It's also good for digestion and is a mild laxative, and it can be used as a gargle to ease a sore throat.

The pulp has a fruity aroma and is both high in acid and sugar. It is used widely as an acidifying agent – much like lemon or lime – in soups, curries, salads and sweet dishes. Its high pectin content makes it useful for jams and chutneys, too. It's also used to make a refreshing drink, which in some countries is carbonated.

Tamarind is sold in a slab with seeds and fibre. Break off a lump of tamarind and soak it in hot water. When the water is cool, break it apart with the fingers, massage the stones to release the pulp, then pass the pulp through a sieve to catch the seeds and fibre. Prepared tamarind will keep for a week or more in a container in the fridge, or it can be frozen; freezing it in small amounts is a good idea. Ice-cube trays are ideal and most trays make cubes that equal 1 tablespoon of pulp. Store unused tamarind well wrapped in the door of the refrigerator.

Tomatoes
Tomatoes need lots of sun to develop a full, sweet flavour. Sun-ripened on the vine, outdoor tomatoes have much more flavour than indoor tomatoes. Italian canned tomatoes generally have a good vibrant orangey-red colour, a meaty texture with few seeds, thick (not watery) juice, and a sweet, fruity taste – they taste as if they've been packed with sunshine.

Lycopene – the antioxidant phytochemical found in tomatoes – is linked with reducing the risk of prostate cancer and appears beneficial in reducing the spread of some skin cancers and in coronary heart disease. The level of lycopene in tomatoes increases when tomatoes are cooked; whole fresh tomatoes contain half the amount found in canned tomatoes.

Including cooked tomatoes in your diet on a regular basis is highly recommended and canned tomatoes are as good as any others. Fat helps the body absorb lycopene so Italian pasta sauces made with canned tomatoes and olive oil, which brings other benefits to the diet, are an enjoyable way of taking your culinary medicine!

When tomatoes are eaten raw, there's usually no need to remove the skin unless they are tough. But if you are using fresh tomatoes in soups, sauces or vegetable stews, it's wise to peel them first; the skin tends to separate from the flesh during cooking and float to the surface. It develops a tough texture and looks unappetising and cooked tomato skins are not easily digested.

To peel tomatoes, drop them into a saucepan of boiling water and leave for 12–20 seconds, depending on how ripe they are. Lift out the tomatoes with a slotted spoon and transfer to a bowl of cold water. If a tomato is difficult to peel, repeat the process. If the tomato looks fluffy or furry, it was in the water for too long and has started to cook; reduce the time for the next lot of tomatoes.

Keep tomatoes at room temperature, not in the refrigerator; chilling tomatoes ruins both their texture and taste.

Vanilla extract

Vanilla essence is a cheap imitation of pure vanilla extract, which is made from real vanilla.

Vanilla pods

Vanilla pods have plenty of flavour and can be reused several times – just as well, as good pods are expensive. If infusing custards and creams with a vanilla pod, rinse the pod thoroughly under running water after use. Dry the pod on a piece of paper towel on a sunny windowsill, until it is thoroughly dry. It will still have plenty of flavour so store it in a cool dry place in an airtight container. Alternatively, imbed it in a jar of caster sugar and use the flavoured sugar in baking.

Vegetables, cooking

Vegetables that grow above ground are exposed to light and the changes in the weather and don't need such cosseted cooking as root vegetables or those that grow underground. Plunge them into boiling water to shorten the cooking time and help set their bright colours. Cook the vegetables at a gentle, not fierce, boil – rapid boiling can cause them to break up. Cook vegetables without a lid because it's best to allow vegetable acids to be driven off in steam rather than collecting under a lid and dripping back onto the vegetables to cause discolouration and an unpleasant odour.

Vegetables that grow underground should be put in a saucepan and covered with cold water and slowly brought to the boil. They have a denser structure – compare a potato with a green bean or a pea. If denser vegetables are plunged into boiling water and boiled fast, the outside structure softens before the heat has a chance to penetrate to the centre and the outside will be overcooked before the centre gets tender. Cooking gently ensures even cooking.

Worcestershire sauce

This strongly flavoured sauce – also known as Worcester sauce – probably originated in the 1840s. A barrel of spice vinegar made to order for a customer using an Indian recipe was never collected from Lea Perrin's chemist shop in Worcester. It was left for some years in the cellar where it began to ferment, probably because it contained soy sauce. The shopkeeper decided to taste it before throwing it out, liked what he tasted, bottled it and sold it off as sauce . . . the rest is history. It's now used throughout the world, and is particularly popular in Japan and China.

weights and measures

Grams to ounces and vice versa

GENERAL			EXACT		
30g	=	1oz	1oz	=	28.35g
60g	=	2oz	2oz	=	56.70g
90g	=	3oz	3oz	=	85.05g
120g	=	4oz	4oz	=	113.04g
150g	=	5oz	5oz	=	141.08g
180g	=	6oz	6oz	=	170.01g
210g	=	7oz	7oz	=	198.04g
230g	=	8oz	8oz	=	226.08g
260g	=	9oz	9oz	=	255.01g
290g	=	10oz	10oz	=	283.05g
320g	=	11oz	11oz	=	311.08g
350g	=	12oz	12oz	=	340.02g
380g	=	13oz	13oz	=	368.05g
410g	=	14oz	14oz	=	396.09g
440g	=	15oz	15oz	=	425.02g
470g	=	16oz	16oz	=	453.06g

Recipes based on these (international units) rounded values

Liquid measurements

25ml	(28.4ml)	=	1fl oz					
150ml	(142ml)	=	5fl oz	=	¼ pint	=	1 gill
275ml	(284ml)	=	10fl oz	=	½ pint		
425ml	(426ml)	=	15fl oz	=	¾ pint		
575ml	(568ml)	=	20fl oz	=	1 pint		

Spoon measures

¼ teaspoon	=	1.25ml
½ teaspoon	=	2.5ml
1 teaspoon	=	5ml
1 tablespoon	=	15ml

In NZ, SA, USA and UK 1 tablespoon = 15ml

In Australia 1 tablespoon = 20ml

1 tablespoon butter = about 10g

Measurements

cm to approx inches

0.5cm	=	¼ in	5cm	=	2 in
1.25cm	=	½ in	7.5cm	=	3 in
2.5cm	=	1 in	10cm	=	4 in

Oven temperatures

CELSIUS	FAHRENHEIT	GAS	
110°C	225°F	¼	very cool
120°C	250°F	½	
140°C	275°F	1	cool
150°C	300°F	2	
170°C	325°F	3	moderate
180°C	350°F	4	
190°C	375°F	5	moderately hot
200°C	400°F	6	
220°C	425°F	7	hot
230°C	450°F	8	
240°C	475°F	9	very hot

Abbreviations

g	gram
kg	kilogram
mm	millimetre
cm	centimetre
ml	millilitre
tsp	teaspoon
Tbsp	tablespoon
°C	degrees Celsius
°F	degrees Fahrenheit

American imperial

in	inch
lb	pound
oz	ounce

index

A

aïoli, Best-ever steak and tomato sandwich with   46
Apple buttermilk hotcakes   16
asparagus
   Barbecued asparagus   129
   Bruschetta with asparagus and prosciutto   56
   Toasted asparagus rolls   29
aubergines (eggplants)
   Aubergine and white bean salad   130
   Couscous with aubergine   93
   Grilled aubergine rolls stuffed with feta   41
   Lamb and aubergine salad with chickpeas and roasted tomatoes   90
   Mozzarella and chargrilled aubergine stack   54
   Smoky aubergine purée   30
avocados
   Avocados and pawns with lime and tomato salsa   35
   Barbecued sweet corn salad with semi-dried tomatoes and avocado   133
   Bruschetta with guacamole and crispy bacon   63
   Crunchy potato cakes with avocado salsa   23
   Gazpacho with avocado and prawns   31
   Smoked fish, avocado and orange on bruschetta   59

B

bacon
   Bacon and egg butties   54
   Bruschetta with guacamole and crispy bacon   63
   Crispy bacon rolls with walnuts and tamarillo chutney   42

Banana hotcakes   12
Barbecued asparagus   129
Barbecued fish on crushed jersey bennes   112
Barbecued lamb tacos   116
Barbecued sweet corn salad with semi-dried tomatoes and avocado   133
barbecuing, know-how   160–161
Beach-side salad   124
beef
   Beef satay   70
   Beef, yellow peppers and shallots on sticks   85
   Best-ever steak and tomato sandwich with aïoli   46
   Chilli beef with lime and palm sugar dressing   88
   Gourmet beef burgers   62
   Korean beef and lettuce cups   42
   Speedy beef stir-fry   100
beetroot
   Bruschetta with baby beetroot, goat's cheese and toasted walnuts   49
berries
   Berry macaroon creams   159
   Buttermilk hotcakes with raspberries and strawberries   156
   Coffee and chocolate cream with raspberries   157
   Quick strawberry trifles   152
Best-ever steak and tomato sandwich with aïoli   46
bruschetta
   Bruschetta with asparagus and prosciutto   56
   Bruschetta with baby beetroot, goat's cheese and toasted walnuts   49
   Bruschetta with guacamole and crispy bacon   63

   Bruschetta with spanish beans, broad beans and sizzled ham   60
   Smoked fish, avocado and orange on bruschetta   59
Buttermilk hotcakes with raspberries and strawberries   156

C

capsicums – see peppers
Chicken
   Chicken and pineapple skewers with pomegranate molasses   84
   Chicken breasts on the barbie with tomato salsa   111
   Chicken lollipops 68
   Chicken satay   75
   Greek chicken kebabs   81
   Green chicken curry with cashew nuts   94
   Green mango and smoked chicken salad with cellophane noodles   101
   Grilled chicken sandwiches with rouille and roasted tomatoes   50
   Indonesian chicken cakes with tomato chilli sauce   121
   Spicy chicken skewers   80
   Tabbouleh with panfried chicken tenderloins   105
chilli
   Chilli beef with lime and palm sugar dressing   88
   Chilli dipping sauce   144
   Indonesian chicken cakes with tomato chilli sauce   121
   Spicy chilli dressing   140
chutney
   Coriander and coconut chutney   142
   Crispy bacon rolls with walnuts and tamarillo chutney   42
Coffee and chocolate cream with raspberries   157

Coriander and coconut chutney   142
Couscous with aubergine   93
crab
    Mini Thai crab cakes   36
Crispy bacon rolls with walnuts and
    tamarillo chutney   42
Crunchy potato cakes with avocado
    salsa   23
cucumber
    Cucumber and pineapple sambal
    146
    Cucumber mayonnaise dip   146
    Fish cakes with cucumber relish   117
    Lamb salad with bean sprouts and
    cucumber   104

D
dressings
    Chilli beef with lime and palm sugar
    dressing   88
    Shallot vinaigrette   145
    Spicy chilli dressing   140

E
Easy coffee semifreddo   154
eggs
    Bacon and egg butties   54
    Egg in the hole   15
    Isanna's eggs on ciabatta   55
eggplant – see aubergine

F
Fattoush   126
feta cheese
    Barbecued pepper and feta salad
    129
    Grilled aubergine rolls stuffed with
    feta   41
    Salad of green beans, rocket and
    feta   130
    Seared vine tomatoes with feta   103
Fish
    Barbecued fish on crushed jersey
    bennes   112
    Fish cakes with cucumber relish   117
    Fish kebabs on warm tomatoes   83
    Rosemary skewers of monkfish and
    scallops   78
    Smoked fish, avocado and orange
    on bruschetta   59
    Summer fish   96
    Vietnamese herb salad with fish   98
Fluffy pancakes with maple syrup   157
Fresh apricot trifle   152
Fresh cherry trifle   154
Fresh sausage rolls   15

Fresh tomato salsa   141
fruit – see also specific fruits
    Apple buttermilk hotcakes   16
    Banana hotcakes   12
    Berry macaroon creams   159
    Buttermilk hotcakes with raspberries
    and strawberries   156
    Coffee and chocolate cream with
    raspberries   157
    Fresh apricot trifle   152
    Fresh cherry trifle   154
    Gingernut creams with pears   159
    Golden kiwifruit salsa   144
    Quick strawberry trifles   152
    Raisin bread with ricotta, honey and
    barbecued peaches   10
    Roasted plums with lavender petals
    156

G
Gazpacho with avocado and prawns
    31
Gingernut creams with pears   159
Golden kiwifruit salsa   144
Gourmet beef burgers   62
Greek chicken kebabs   81
Green chicken curry with cashew nuts
    94
Green mango and smoked chicken
    salad with cellophane noodles   101
Grilled aubergine rolls stuffed with
    feta   41
Grilled chicken sandwiches with rouille
    and roasted tomatoes   50
Grilled pizza   62
Grilled squid salad   96

H
Hash cakes   12
Hot and sour pork   97
hotcakes
    Apple buttermilk hotcakes   16
    Banana hotcakes   12
    Buttermilk hotcakes with raspberries
    and strawberries   156
Huevos con patatas   20

I
Indonesian chicken cakes with tomato
    chilli sauce   121
Isanna's eggs on ciabatta   55

K
Kachumbar   132
Korean beef and lettuce cups   42

L
lamb
    Barbecued lamb tacos   116
    Lamb and aubergine salad with
    chickpeas and roasted tomatoes   90
    Lamb cutlets with grilled red peppers
    114
    Lamb salad with bean sprouts and
    cucumber   104
    Lamburgers with middle-eastern
    flavours   64
lemon
    Lemon and elderflower granita   150
    Pork patties with fennel seeds and
    lemon   120
    Tomatoes with lemon zest   20
lime
    Avocados and pawns with lime and
    tomato salsa   35
    Chilli beef with lime and palm sugar
    dressing   88
    Prawns with crushed lemon grass
    and kaffir lime leaves   81
Lollipop chicken   68

M
mangoes
    Green mango and smoked chicken
    salad with cellophane noodles   101
    Mango honey salsa   145
    Mango salsa   142
Meatballs wrapped in lemon leaves
    116
Mini Thai crab cakes   36
Mozzarella and chargrilled aubergine
    stack   54
Muhammara   140
mushrooms
    Portobello mushrooms with
    prosciutto and balsamic vinegar   52

O
orange
    Orange and red onion salad   134
    Smoked fish, avocado and orange on
    bruschetta   59

P
Pan-fried calamari with lemon pepper
    mayonnaise   32
peppers (capsicum)
    Barbecued pepper and feta salad   129
    Beef, yellow peppers and shallots on
    sticks   85
    Lamb cutlets with grilled red peppers
    114

Muhammara   140
Pesto dip with roasted red pepper and olives   30
Pesto dip with roasted red pepper and olives   30
pineapple
Chicken and pineapple skewers with pomegranate molasses   84
Cucumber and pineapple sambal   146
pork – see also bacon, prosciutto
Hot and sour pork   97
Meatballs wrapped in lemon leaves   116
Pork balls   112
Pork chops with lychees and micro salad   118
Pork patties with fennel seeds and lemon   120
Pork satay   72
Vietnamese pork balls with fresh herb salad   103
Portobello mushrooms with prosciutto and balsamic vinegar   52
potatoes
Barbecued fish on crushed jersey bennes   112
Crunchy potato cakes with avocado salsa   23
Hash cakes   12
Huevos con patatas   20
prawns
Gazpacho with avocado and prawns   31
Prawn and chorizo bites   38
Prawn skewers   80
Prawns and scallops on skewers   76
Prawns with crushed lemon grass and kaffir lime leaves   81
Spicy prawns in green coats   26
Thai prawn and noodle salad   104
Tiger prawns with mixed leaf salad and sizzled lychees   84
prosciutto
Bruschetta with asparagus and prosciutto   56
Portobello mushrooms with prosciutto and balsamic vinegar   52

Q
Quesadillas   18
Quick strawberry trifles   152

R
Raisin bread with ricotta, honey and barbecued peaches   10

Roasted plums with lavender petals   156
Roasted tomato sauce with honey and cinnamon   139
Rosemary skewers of monkfish and scallops   78

S
salads
Aubergine and white bean salad   130
Barbecued pepper and feta salad   129
Barbecued sweet corn salad with semi-dried tomatoes and avocado   133
Beach-side salad   124
Fattoush   126
Kachumbar   132
Lamb salad with bean sprouts and cucumber   104
Orange and red onion salad   134
Salad of green beans, rocket and feta   130
Thai prawn and noodle salad   104
Tiger prawns with mixed leaf salad and sizzled lychees   84
Tomato and mint salad   124
Vietnamese herb salad with fish   98
Vietnamese pork balls with fresh herb salad   103
salsa
Avocados and pawns with lime and tomato salsa   35
Chicken breasts on the barbie with tomato salsa   111
Crunchy potato cakes with avocado salsa   23
Fresh tomato salsa   141
Golden kiwifruit salsa   144
Mango honey salsa   145
Mango salsa   142
Smoky tomato salsa   141
sausage rolls, Fresh   15
scallops
Prawns and scallops on skewers   76
Rosemary skewers of monkfish and scallops   78
Scallops with guacamole   38
Seared scallops on warm fregola salad   100
Seared scallops on warm fregola salad   100
Seared vine tomatoes with feta   103
Shallot vinaigrette   145
Smoked fish, avocado and orange on

bruschetta   59
Smoky aubergine purée   30
Smoky tomato salsa   141
Speedy beef stir-fry   100
Spicy chicken skewers   80
Spicy chilli dressing   140
Spicy prawns in green coats   26
Spicy satay sauce   144
squid
Grilled squid salad   96
steak – see beef
Summer fish   96
sweet corn
Barbecued sweet corn salad with semi-dried tomatoes and avocado   133

T
Tabbouleh with panfried chicken tenderloins   105
Thai prawn and noodle salad   104
Tiger prawns with mixed leaf salad and sizzled lychees   84
Toasted asparagus rolls   29
tomatoes
Barbecued sweet corn salad with semi-dried tomatoes and avocado   133
Best-ever steak and tomato sandwich with aïoli   46
Chicken breasts on the barbie with tomato salsa   111
Fish kebabs on warm tomatoes   83
Fresh tomato salsa   141
Grilled chicken sandwiches with rouille and roasted tomatoes   50
Indonesian chicken cakes with tomato chilli sauce   121
Roasted tomato sauce with honey and cinnamon   139
Seared vine tomatoes with feta   103
Smoky tomato salsa   141
Tomato and mint salad   124
Tomatoes with lemon zest   20
tuna
Tuna fish cakes   120
Tuna steaks with tuna fish mayonnaise   108

V
Vietnamese herb salad with fish   98
Vietnamese pork balls with fresh herb salad   103
vinaigrette, Shallot   145

acknowledgements

Thanks and acknowledgements to a great team.

You excelled yourself on this book, Aaron (McLean, photographer), capturing my vision but adding your own creative spark. A great job. Julie Wyatt (stylist), thanks for making the photographs looks so gorgeous with perfect props. My family is always an essential part of my books. Thanks Remo, Luca and Ilaria for being so wildly enthusiastic about critiquing the food – even if it was driven by hunger! Remo, too, for all the thousands of jobs done behind the scenes including food preparation, photography assistance and general organisation. To my brother Colin and wife Jenny, a huge thanks for being my greatest supporters and for always producing a chilled savvie just at the right moment! My old friends (and getting older!) Joanne, Liz and Richard, Jean and Norman, Roger and Tessa, and Marg – what can I say but thanks for the fun and camaraderie, the encouragement, the help, the suggestions, and of course for sharing your good food with me, too. To my American friends: Ron, thanks for your boundless energy, endless suggestions and gifted inspiration, and Mark, too, for being such a great friend. And a special thanks to Robin Ward for all her associated work on my website www.juliebiuso.com.

To my dear, dear friends, Ray & Barbara Richards, thanks for being such special people in my life. To my friend and publisher Belinda Cooke, a huge thanks for running with this project when the rest of the world was collapsing around our ears. Also from New Holland, a big thanks to Matt Turner, Dee Murch and Margaret Kaye. Thanks also to editors Fiona McRae and Louise Armstrong.

The subject matter for this book was right up designer Christine Hansen's alley, being a lover of the sea, sun and outdoor life. This one's a cracker, Christine! And thanks, too, to Lorraine Steele, publicist, it's a big ask to get a book moving in these times, but you did it!

I'd also like to acknowledge the two ACP magazines I write for and their editors. Suzanne Dale, editor of *Taste* magazine and Leanne Moore, editor of *Your Home & Garden* magazine. Many of the recipes in this book had their first run in these magazines. Thanks, to both of you, for always being so enthusiastic about my work and for all your support.

And finally, I'd like to acknowledge the following companies for their help:

Freedom Farms www.freedomfarms.co.nz
Gourmet Direct www.gourmetdirect.com
Robin Ward www.webmontage.com
Artedomus www.artedomus.co.nz
Corso de` Fiori www.corso.co.nz
Country Road www.countryroad.co.nz
Cranfields www.cranfields.com
Glengarry Hancocks www.hancocks.co.nz
Japanese Lifestyle www.japanlife.co.nz
Junk & Disorderly www.junkndisorderly.co.nz
Middle Earth Tile & Design www.middleearthtiles.co.nz
Nest www.nest.co.nz
Republic Home www.republichome.com
The Poi Room www.thepoiroom.co.nz
Urban Loft wwwurbanloft.co.nz

First published in 2009 by
New Holland Publishers (NZ) Ltd
Auckland • Sydney • London • Cape Town

www.newhollandpublishers.co.nz

218 Lake Road, Northcote, Auckland 0627,
New Zealand
Unit 1, 66 Gibbes Street, Chatswood, NSW 2067,
Australia
86–88 Edgware Road, London W2 2EA,
United Kingdom
80 McKenzie Street, Cape Town 8001, South Africa

ISBN: 978 1 86966 249 3

Commissioned by Belinda Cooke
Publishing manager: Matt Turner
Editors: Fiona McRae and Louise Armstrong
Design: Christine Hansen

A catalogue record for this book is available from
the National Library of New Zealand.

10 9 8 7 6 5 4 3 2 1

Printed in China by SNP Leefung on paper sourced
from sustainable forests.